Raising Arizona's Dams

A. E. Rogge

D. Lorne McWatters

Melissa Keane

Richard P. Emanuel

Raising

Arizona's Dams

Daily Life, Danger, and Discrimination in the Dam Construction Camps of Central Arizona, 1890s–1940s

The University of Arizona Press   Tucson & London

Publication of this book was funded in part by the U.S. Department of the Interior, Bureau of Reclamation, Phoenix Area Office, under contracts 6-CS-30-04360 and 4-FC-32-00230.

Frontispiece: Roosevelt Dam, circa 1916 (Postcard from Melissa Keane collection)

The University of Arizona Press
Copyright © 1995
The Arizona Board of Regents

☉ This book is printed on acid-free, archival-quality paper.

00 99 98 97 96 95   6 5 4 3 2 1

 LIBRARY OF CONGRESS CATALOGING-IN-PUBLICATION DATA
Raising Arizona's dams : daily life, danger, and discrimination in the dam construction camps of central Arizona, 1890s–1940s / by A. E. Rogge . . . [et al.].
   p.   cm.
   Includes bibliographical references and index.
   ISBN 0-8165-1491-7 (alk. paper). —
   ISBN 0-8165-1492-5 (pbk. : alk. paper)
   1. Construction workers—Arizona—History. 2. Dams—Arizona—History. 3. Irrigation engineering—Arizona—History. 4. Arizona—Social conditions. 5. Cities and towns—Arizona—History. 6. Arizona—History.   I. Rogge, A. E.
HD8039.B92U667   1995   94-21368
331.7'6278'09791—dc20   CIP
British Cataloguing-in-Publication Data
A catalogue record for this book is available from the British Library.

To those who wore "blue collars"
        before the phrase was coined

Contents

Figures

Preface

The Central Arizona Project is designed to import waters from the Colorado River into the desert of central and southern Arizona, where most of the state's farms and cities are located. In 1968, Congress authorized the Bureau of Reclamation to construct this massive water development project. Although some elements of the project were still under construction, the Bureau of Reclamation declared the project substantially complete in 1993 and directed the Central Arizona Water Conservation District to begin repaying the costs of the project (at subsidized interest rates). The District, organized to operate and maintain the canals, pumping plants, and dams, will continue to make installment payments over the next half century. The Central Arizona Project is a continuation of federal government reclamation policies that date back almost a century, but it is also one of the last big reclamation projects the federal government will build.

One element of the Central Arizona Project was a proposed Orme Dam, which was to be built at the confluence of the Salt and Verde rivers to store irrigation water and control floods. When a draft environmental impact statement for the proposed Orme Dam was released in the mid-1970s, numerous public concerns were voiced about such issues as the destruction of bald eagle habitat and the inundation of two-thirds of the Fort McDowell Indian Reservation. The Bureau of Reclamation reacted by studying ways to achieve water supply and flood control without Orme Dam, and the agency came up with nine alternatives. In 1982, after lengthy review, the secretary of the interior chose the sixth alternative. "Plan 6" involves raising the height of Roosevelt Dam by more than seventy feet, replacing Waddell Dam, modifying Stewart Mountain Dam, and strengthening other dams on the Salt and Verde rivers. Plan 6 also originally included construction of Cliff Dam to replace Horseshoe Dam, but this element of the plan was subsequently dropped.

Construction activities and the enlarged reservoirs of Plan 6 threatened to damage or destroy archaeological and historical sites. To offset this, the Bureau of Reclamation contracted teams of archaeologists and historians to survey, research, and report on threatened sites. Hundreds of sites were found and recorded. Most were remnants of the prehistoric cultures that had occupied the river valleys centuries and millennia ago, but some were much younger sites from the historic era. Many of these were remnants of the vanished camps where laborers lived while building the dams that are now being modified or replaced. The archaeological and historical investigation of those temporary worker communities is the subject of this book.

Acknowledgments

This book is a spinoff of the Plan 6 Historical Archaeological Project, which was funded by the Bureau of Reclamation. We gratefully acknowledge the support of the agency and, in particular, the encouragement of Tom Lincoln, who served as technical monitor for the study contract.

Historical archaeology is never the undertaking of lone scholars. We four authors owe much to the other members of the Plan 6 project team. Cindy Myers, as coprincipal investigator, helped set the course of the study and devoted her energy and enthusiasm to the project during the initial, hectic years. Everett Bassett was field director for the project and bore major responsibility for making the many day-to-day decisions of archaeological fieldwork. He also was the first to recognize the archaeological evidence of the Apache laborer camps, and he undertook much of the research examining the role of Apaches in the Roosevelt Dam project. Jim Ayres served as the chief artifact analyst for the project. Our studies could never have been completed without his expertise in identifying the thousands of collected artifacts.

Many other colleagues made significant contributions along the way. Cultural anthropologist and linguist Dr. Elizabeth Brandt was particularly helpful with the oral history of Apache involvement at Roosevelt. Archaeologist Alan Ferg volunteered his knowledge, efforts, and enthusiasm in the nascent field of Apache archaeology. Sociologist Dr. Phylis Martinelli shared her insight into issues of ethnicity and her familiarity with the Italian community in central Arizona. Historian David Introcaso was a source of information about the history of water resource development in central Arizona, and historian Dr. Karen Smith facilitated our use of the Salt River Project archives. We also acknowledge the cooperation of the staff at other repositories, including the Arizona Department of Library, Archives, and Public Records; the Arizona Historical Foundation; the Arizona Historical Society; and the Arizona Room of the Hayden Library at Arizona State University. We thank Dorothy McLaughlin and the late Herb McLaughlin for granting access to a part of their vast historical photograph collection, which was a remarkable resource for reconstructing the history of Camp Pleasant. Fritz Seifritz, ranger at the Lake Pleasant County Park, also freely shared his knowledge of the area, along with photographs and maps he had collected, and tips about potential sources of oral history.

We spoke with approximately two dozen people about their memories of dam construction camps. We owe them all a great debt of thanks, but we especially acknowledge the cooperation of Frank Cutter, Elmer Horton, Joaquin Imperial, and Lee and Ray Price as key sources of information.

We owe a primary debt to the members of the field and laboratory crews of the Plan 6 project, without whom the archaeological data would never have been collected and analyzed. Those stalwart souls included Lisa Champagne, Ross Curtis, Diane Fenicle, Leta Franklin, Noreen Fritz, Carol Griffith, Jeff Hathaway, Lynette Heller, Deborah Hull-Walski, Jason Jones, Simon Krauss, Sue Lewenstein, Sarah Millspaugh, Penny Minturn, Pamela Patterson, Brenda Randolph, Ron Savage, Chris Schrager, Kelly Schroder, Dawn Snell, James Tyler, and Frank Walski. Dr. Stan Hordes and Dr. Michael Scardaville provided advice and assistance in the identification and analysis of historical materials, and Fred Anderson, Dennis Preisler, and Linda Sellers ably assisted as historical document sleuths.

Glenn Darrington, Kristie James, Mitch Meek, Ron Savage, and Shirley Wiley helped with the production of graphics and tables and the "processing" of words. Dr. Simon Bruder unselfishly took on extra burdens to free us to work on this project.

Last, we are indebted to the able staff of the University of Arizona Press, who helped us move the project toward publication.

Without the help of all these individuals, and the many unnamed others, we never would have been able to tell the story we relate in this book. Although many individuals, organizations, and agencies contributed, only we are responsible for the judgments and interpretations made in reconstructing this history.

Raising Arizona's Dams

1

Watering the West

Water, or its lack, has shaped every aspect of America's desert Southwest. Towering saguaros and tiny scorpions are remarkably well adapted to the region's heat and aridity. The echoing Grand Canyon continues to be carved into the earth by the waters of the Colorado River. In the Southwest, water has shaped human history and culture as profoundly as the landscape.

The Southwest has not always been desert. Twelve thousand years ago, late in the Pleistocene glacial epoch, the Paleo-Indians who moved into what is now Arizona enjoyed more abundant rainfall and a comparatively mild climate. As the Ice Age relaxed its grip on the planet, the region warmed and rainfall declined. Eventually, the hot, arid climate of today's desert emerged. With some fluctuations, the Sonoran Desert of Arizona and northern Mexico has persisted for the last ten thousand years.

About two thousand years ago, a people whom archaeologists call the Hohokam took the first steps toward modifying Arizona's desert environment. Turning from the region's nomadic hunting and gathering economy, they began to raise desert-adapted crops. They settled into upland villages and moved into the valleys, where they built extensive systems of irrigation canals. By A.D. 700, the Hohokam were managing vast systems of hand-dug canals, as large as fifty to seventy-five

The idea that nature has had something to do with the shaping of cultures and history is an idea that is both obviously true and persistently neglected.
—Donald Worster
(1985:22)

feet across and extending up to twenty miles across the dry desert (Haury 1976; Howard and Huckleberry 1991; Masse 1981). More than five hundred miles of main canals irrigated 25,000 acres of cropland in the Salt River Valley alone (Doyel 1991).

The Hohokam were among the most sophisticated irrigators in all of the prehistoric New World, flourishing for centuries after they began to water the desert. They grew corn, cotton, beans, squash, and tobacco, and by A.D. 1100 had established dozens of villages, the greatest boasting perhaps a thousand people (Doyel 1991). While European kings and nobles vied to forge medieval alliances, Hohokam traders exported textiles, pigments, and other desert resources south into Mesoamerica in exchange for marine shells, copper bells, tropical birds, and other prized goods.

However, by A.D. 1400, Hohokam civilization had largely vanished. Many villages lay abandoned, and the neglected canals began to fill with sediment. The cause of the Hohokam decline remains a puzzle, but most archaeologists suspect an environmental catastrophe—a disastrous flood, a prolonged drought, or soils laden with salt after centuries of irrigation. One way or another, most theories involve water, although social problems including intertribal warfare may also have played a role (Noble 1991). Whatever the cause, the demise of the Hohokam set a pattern in the Phoenix basin: agriculture, irrigation, urbanization, eclipse. The pattern began to be repeated in the 1860s at a much faster pace, but modern Phoenicians hope they will escape the pattern's final phase.

After the fall of Hohokam civilization, American Indians continued to live throughout what is now Arizona. Spanish conquistadors and missionaries who first probed the area in the sixteenth century found a variety of distinct native cultures. None, however, had the complex social structures and dense populations of the vanished Hohokam (Haury 1945; Winters 1973).

Spanish hegemony brought no real advances in harnessing Arizona's water resources beyond those achieved by prehistoric technology. Although Spanish water engineering was sophisticated for its time, it was not applied in Arizona, an isolated province of the empire. Mexican rule likewise brought little change, for after its 1821 revolution and break with Spain, the government lacked the wherewithal to settle and occupy its northern frontier.

Change did follow American acquisition of Southwestern land at the end of the Mexican-American War. Most of the future state of Arizona was obtained by treaty in 1848. The rest was purchased six years later, and the pace of settlement quickened. In 1865, the U.S. Army established Fort McDowell along the Verde River just upstream of its confluence with the Salt River, and soldiers dug an irrigation canal to conduct Verde River water to fields near the fort (Wagoner 1970).

At about this time, one of Arizona's more colorful characters, John W. "Jack" Swilling, entered the scene (see "Jack Swilling: Not the First," p. 18). Swilling had been a gold prospector, Indian fighter, Confederate deserter, and Union Army scout by 1867, when he visited John Y. T. "Yours Truly" Smith, who was harvesting wild hay along the Salt River and selling it to the army. According to legend, Swilling is said to have first recognized the ruined remnants of the prehistoric Hohokam irrigation system while reviewing Smith's operation, and he decided to form a company to dig canals to irrigate crops that could be sold to Wickenburg miners and to the army at Camp McDowell.

By December 1867, the Swilling Irrigating and Canal Company was at work in the Salt River Valley, unearthing abandoned Hohokam canals and digging new ditches. The next spring, wheat, corn, and barley were planted in irrigated fields. By the time crops were ready to harvest in the fall of 1868, a hundred people had settled near the canals. Mindful that the community had sprung forth on the ruins of an ancient civilization, someone—perhaps Swilling or an associate, Darrell Duppa—named the new town Phoenix, after the mythical bird of Egypt that arose renewed from its own ashes (Luckingham 1989).

The renewal of irrigation marked a turning point in the history of the Salt River Valley. Within a decade, eleven private companies carried water to customers on both sides of the river through more than twenty canals (Zarbin 1984). In 1882, the Arizona Canal Company began a forty-mile-long canal to tap the Salt River east of Phoenix. Nearly half a millennium after the ancient irrigators had vanished, this canal was the first extension of the prehistoric Hohokam system.

Irrigated farming immediately showed great promise in the Salt River Valley. With good soils and plenty of sun, only water was needed to make the desert bloom, but it took constant care to keep water flowing from the river into the fertile fields. First, a diversion dam, usually of heavy timber, rock, and brush, sent water coursing from the river into a main canal. The canal required the right slope for water to flow by gravity, sometimes tens of miles across the desert. Often a suitable slope was achieved simply by unearthing a buried Hohokam canal. From the main canal, water poured through a headgate into a network of distribution ditches, finally flowing into the furrowed fields (Smith 1987). At every step, maintenance was needed to keep waterways clear and control structures working. Farmers in the Salt River Valley needed only water to work wonders, but they soon learned that wonders were not easily assured.

First Steps Toward Paradise

During the late 1860s, General William Tecumseh Sherman inspected military defenses in the newly established Arizona Territory. A local assured the Civil War hero that all Arizona needed was "less heat and more water." The laconic Sherman replied, "That's all Hell needs."
—Bert M. Fireman (1982:3)

The newcomers who settled in Arizona during the nineteenth century did not at first appreciate how different the rivers of the Southwest are from the streams with which they were familiar. Desert rivers fluctuate wildly in flow from year to year and from season to season, even from day to day. Annual precipitation is low and uneven in central Arizona, where typically half comes in heavy summer cloudbursts. Rocky soils, sparsely covered with vegetation, shed torrents of water into streambeds, often resulting in flash floods. In times of drought, the Salt River carries as little as 200 cubic feet of water per second. After heavy rains, it can swell a thousand times that rate, to 200,000 cubic feet per second. In historic times, the floods of 1891 and 1905 are legendary, as are the most recent flows of 1993 (fig. 1.1) (see "The Great Flood of A.D. 899," p. 20).

Extremes in Arizona rivers posed persistent problems for early farmers and dam builders. When there was no rain, streams dried up, and there was too little water to go around. Bitter disputes broke out over rights to the meager water supply. When the rains came, heavy downpours endangered diversion dams. Northwest of Phoenix, the Walnut Grove Water Storage Company began to build a dam across the Hassayampa River in 1886. After torrential rains, the barely completed dam failed on February 22, 1890, drowning between 70 and 130 people. The dam was never rebuilt (Dill 1987).

In 1885, the Arizona Canal Company completed a diversion dam on the Salt River for its new canal system. The Arizona Dam, a heavy, plank crib filled with rocks, was repeatedly damaged and rebuilt until it was destroyed by a flood after two decades of use. As part of the Roosevelt Dam project, the Arizona Dam was replaced by the concrete Granite Reef Diversion Dam, which has been in service since 1908.

FIGURE 1.1 The men in the foreground are sitting on twisted pieces of the shattered Phoenix and Eastern Railroad bridge, destroyed in a flood in 1891. Another Salt River flood destroyed railroad bridges linking Tempe and Phoenix in 1905. (Courtesy of Herb and Dorothy McLaughlin Historical Collection)

Fortunately, there seemed to be an answer to both of the major problems, drought and flood. Carefully engineered dams could hold back floods and protect downstream structures, while reservoirs could store water for release in times of drought. Then, if conflicting claims to water could be sorted out by the courts, nothing could impede the development of paradise in the Arizona desert.

The Supreme Court of the Arizona Territory took steps to settle confusion over water rights in 1892, when Judge Joseph H. Kibbey issued the now-renowned Kibbey Decision. Kibbey reaffirmed in Arizona the established doctrine of "prior appropriation," the legal basis of water rights in most of the arid West. Prior appropriation is sometimes summarized with the adage, "He who is first in time is first in right." Kibbey applied the doctrine to canal companies in the Salt River Valley to establish the priority of their rights to river flows.

Under prior appropriation, a person's right to use water is determined by the date that person begins to withdraw water. Whoever is first to withdraw water from a source establishes a right to keep withdrawing water at the same rate, even if doing so dries up the source for others. The second person to withdraw has a right superior to the third person, and so on. The doctrine contrasts with water law in wet regions of the United States, where rights to permanent lakes and reliable, year-round rivers belong to all owners of lakeside and riverfront property. In 1910, Judge Edward H. Kent refined the doctrine when he allocated the Salt River's flow to individual parcels of land. The Kent Decree allotted Salt River water rights to farmers based chiefly on the date their fields went into irrigated cultivation.

Setting the basis for parceling out scarce water was important, but legal decisions did nothing to enhance the water supply. For that, dams were needed, and Arizonans turned to the task with a will. In 1892, the year of the Kibbey Decision, a group of entrepreneurs and landowners began an irrigation project on the Agua Fria River, northwest of Phoenix. William Beardsley promoted the Frog Tanks Dam, as it was then called, and initiated construction at the Dyer Diversion Dam. The project was backed by Ohio investors, but the financing collapsed after three years, partly because of an economic recession. The year after work began on the Agua Fria River, another private group joined to promote dams and reservoirs on the Salt River, but even though the Hudson Reservoir and Canal Company spent sizable sums planning dams and working to attract Eastern investment, the group's projects never advanced beyond the planning stage.

The boundless enthusiasm of Western water-development boosters could not alter the fact that robust dams and extensive canal systems are costly to construct. Irrigation promoters found it difficult to raise the needed millions privately, so they began to look to the government for help. At an 1893 irrigation conference in Los Angeles, delegates met in halls bedecked with red, white, and blue bunting to hear speakers proclaim the wonders that waited to be worked with water—if only Washington would build the vital dams. " 'Oh glorious land!' exulted a choir before the conferees. 'Oh glorious land, where fruits purple, crimson, and golden roll forth from plenty's horn!' " (Worster 1985:132).

However, one speaker, although he favored Western development, warned that there was not enough water in the arid

lands to irrigate everywhere. The speaker was John Wesley
Powell, and it was his last public pronouncement on settling the
West. The firestorm of reaction to his scientifically accurate but
politically incautious speech led to Powell's resignation from
his position as head of the U.S. Geological Survey. He retreated
to the relatively obscure Bureau of American Ethnology, which
he had directed since 1879 and continued to lead until his
death (see "Power for Science: John Wesley Powell," p. 22).

The Dam-Building Era: Science Bids the Desert to Drink

Partisans of Western water projects finally carried the day in
June 1902, when Congress passed the Reclamation Act that
created the U.S. Reclamation Service, initially as part of the
U.S. Geological Survey (James 1917). The original legislation
was aimed at developing water resources on public lands. However, because most of the land in the Salt River Valley was
private, prominent Arizonans enlisted the aid of President Theodore Roosevelt to convince Congress to permit the Reclamation Service also to undertake projects on private lands.

The storage of flood waters on a large scale is fast coming to be a matter of prime importance in connection with the development of the arid portions of the United States.
—FREDERICK H. NEWELL
(1897:9)

Soon after the act passed, area farmers and business leaders
formed the Salt River Valley Water Users' Association to press
for their piece of the pie, namely, money to build a dam on the
Salt River (Luckingham 1989). In 1904, the two groups signed
a contract. The Reclamation Service agreed to build the dam,
and the water users agreed to repay the agency for the cost of
the dam, estimated to be $2 million, over ten years at no interest
(Smith 1986).

Roosevelt Dam, as the dam on the upper Salt River became
known, was one of the Reclamation Service's first projects. It
was to be a showcase effort for the new agency, and in most
respects it succeeded, even though it proved to be more costly
than anticipated. Completed in 1911 at a cost of $10 million,
the dam provided water storage and flood control for the Salt
River Valley as well as a modest amount of hydroelectric power.
The massive, stone-block structure impounded more than a
million acre-feet of water in what was then the world's largest
artificial lake, almost ten miles long and two miles wide (Luckingham 1989).

Between 1923 and 1930, three modern concrete-arch
dams—Mormon Flat, Horse Mesa, and Stewart Mountain
dams—also were built on the Salt River, downstream of Roosevelt Dam. They were intended partly to provide additional

water storage and flood control, but mostly to generate more hydroelectric power for sale to pay off government loans for dam construction and, of course, to power further development.

In 1925, William Beardsley's thirty-year crusade to dam the Agua Fria River was reinvigorated, and Lake Pleasant Dam, subsequently renamed Waddell Dam, was erected with private financing. Lake Pleasant was impounded thirty miles northwest of Phoenix, providing water for the Maricopa Water District. The project almost succumbed to concerns over the safety of the dam, a radical design with multiple thin concrete arches. During the Great Depression of the 1930s, funds provided by the federal Reconstruction Finance Corporation allowed the Maricopa Water District to undertake modifications and salvage the project's technological and economic viability (Introcaso 1988).

In the 1930s and 1940s, two dams were built on the Verde River, a tributary of the Salt River, to complement the four existing dams. Bartlett Dam was built to augment the water supply of the Salt River Valley Water Users' Association, but it also provided some water for Salt River Pima Indian lands. Horseshoe Dam was built in accord with a complex agreement that allowed exchanges of water on the upper Salt River for expansion of wartime production at a Phelps Dodge copper mine at Morenci, in eastern Arizona. By 1945, the six dams of the Salt River Project, as the effort had become known, were in place (fig. 1.2). Together they stored about two million acre-feet of water for Salt River Valley lands and generated a considerable amount of hydroelectric power for sale (Smith 1986). Some of the power was used to pump groundwater to supplement surface-water supplies, which were inadequate for the demands of the region's burgeoning cities and farms.

In the 1920s, dams to store and divert water were also built on the Gila River. In 1909, the Reclamation Service completed Laguna Dam to divert Colorado River water near Yuma, but it was not until 1931 that the Bureau of Reclamation embarked on a series of dams and projects to check and store the flows of this mighty "Nile of the West" (Stevens 1988:9). (The U.S. Reclamation Service became independent of the U.S. Geological Survey in 1907 and was renamed the Bureau of Reclamation in 1923 [Worster 1985].) Hoover Dam, completed in 1936 (Stevens 1988), was the first of these structures, followed by Parker Dam and Davis Dam. The latest of the great Colorado

River dams, Glen Canyon Dam, was finished in 1964 (Martin 1989) (fig. 1.3).

Four years later, Congress authorized the Central Arizona Project to divert more of the Colorado River. Now, more than 320 miles of canals, tunnels, and concrete siphons send water from the California border, across Arizona, to slake the thirst of Phoenix and Tucson and the surrounding land (Johnson 1977). The cost of the still-incomplete Central Arizona Project will top $4 billion, making it the largest single undertaking ever attempted by the Bureau of Reclamation (Smith 1986). As the twentieth century draws to a close, reclamation dam building is waning (fig. 1.4), but science and engineering still struggle to live up to the symbolism of bidding the Arizona desert to drink (see "The Symbolism of Watering the West," p. 23).

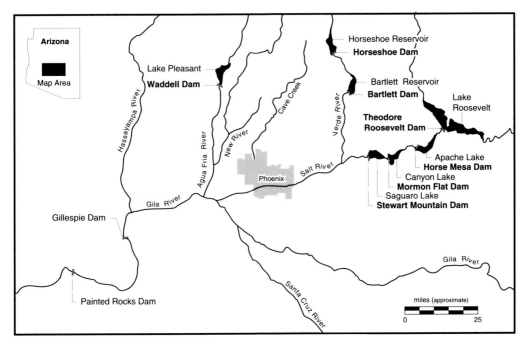

FIGURE 1.2 Historic dam construction camps were studied at each of the seven major reservoirs in central Arizona, but the most abundant archaeological evidence was found at the Waddell and Roosevelt dam locales. (Courtesy of Dames & Moore)

Historical Archaeology: The New History of the Dams

The common folk—not just the movers and the shakers of politics or intellectual life—have a vibrant past and contribute to larger historical processes.
—PETER N. STEARNS
(1983:4)

The seven dams that store water for the arid lands and cities of central Arizona and safeguard them from floods are most commonly recognized by modern urban dwellers as recreational lakes. Most Salt River Valley residents know few details about the history of these dams, although scholars have documented the political history and economic importance of these dams in the development of the state. Waddell Dam, Lake Pleasant, and Roosevelt Dam are named for men with prominent roles in water development in the Salt River Valley, and Jack Swilling's legendary rediscovery of the lost Hohokam canals is familiar to anyone acquainted with Arizona history. However, if history tells only the deeds of great men, it tells only part of the story. At Roosevelt Dam, Theodore Roosevelt laid no blocks of stone, and at Waddell Dam, Donald Waddell arranged for financing but built no concrete forms, and engineer Carl Pleasant hefted blueprints but mixed no concrete.

Mythologized tales of great men tend to leave things out. They overlook such details as the din in the sluicing tunnel at Roosevelt Dam and the vapor-laden steam heat that choked workers excavating the shaft. Two men died constructing the hellish sluicing tunnel (Leighton 1906:134; Zarbin 1984:93). Then too, mythologized histories tend to discount the roles—sometimes even the very presence—of women and minorities. To be sure, histories of Roosevelt Dam generally mention that Apaches labored on the new roads needed for dam construction, but the descriptions of their contributions invariably seem vague and insubstantial, casting them as bit players on the grand stage of the history of Roosevelt Dam. Although State Route 88 has been named the Apache Trail, few realize that Apache laborers actually built the road.

Reconstructions of the past are based on facts, and those who would distort history with hoaxes are sooner or later revealed by other scholars. However, facts are perceived and take on meaning only in an interpretive framework, and these frameworks and the resulting images of the past evolve as scholarly traditions come and go. Historians of the American West have subscribed to at least three major paradigms (August 1986; Worster 1985).

In the 1890s, Frederick Jackson Turner (1985) espoused a frontier model, arguing that the advancement of Euro-American settlement from the Atlantic seaboard west, to open

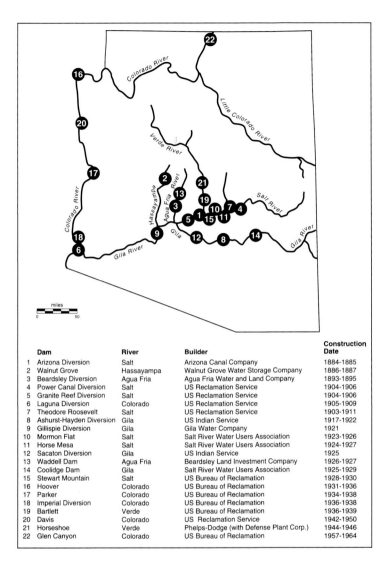

	Dam	River	Builder	Construction Date
1	Arizona Diversion	Salt	Arizona Canal Company	1884-1885
2	Walnut Grove	Hassayampa	Walnut Grove Water Storage Company	1886-1887
3	Beardsley Diversion	Agua Fria	Agua Fria Water and Land Company	1893-1895
4	Power Canal Diversion	Salt	US Reclamation Service	1904-1906
5	Granite Reef Diversion	Salt	US Reclamation Service	1904-1906
6	Laguna Diversion	Colorado	US Reclamation Service	1905-1909
7	Theodore Roosevelt	Salt	US Reclamation Service	1903-1911
8	Ashurst-Hayden Diversion	Gila	US Indian Service	1917-1922
9	Gillispie Diversion	Gila	Gila Water Company	1921
10	Mormon Flat	Salt	Salt River Water Users Association	1923-1926
11	Horse Mesa	Salt	Salt River Water Users Association	1924-1927
12	Sacaton Diversion	Gila	US Indian Service	1925
13	Waddell Dam	Agua Fria	Beardsley Land Investment Company	1926-1927
14	Coolidge Dam	Gila	Salt River Water Users Association	1925-1929
15	Stewart Mountain	Salt	US Bureau of Reclamation	1928-1930
16	Hoover	Colorado	US Bureau of Reclamation	1931-1936
17	Parker	Colorado	US Bureau of Reclamation	1934-1938
18	Imperial Diversion	Colorado	US Bureau of Reclamation	1936-1938
19	Bartlett	Verde	US Bureau of Reclamation	1936-1939
20	Davis	Colorado	US Reclamation Service	1942-1950
21	Horseshoe	Verde	Phelps-Dodge (with Defense Plant Corp.)	1944-1946
22	Glen Canyon	Colorado	US Bureau of Reclamation	1957-1964

FIGURE 1.3 Most of the early dam-building efforts focused on the Salt and Gila river systems of Arizona. Only later did engineers attempt to block and store the waters of the much larger Colorado River. (Courtesy of Dames & Moore)

lands with abundant natural resources, shaped the spirit of not only the West, but the entire nation. According to Turner's model, this frontier experience created an American character that is coarse and strong, inquisitive and practical (rather than artistic), and above all, individualistic and democratic.

In the 1930s, Walter Prescott Webb (1931, 1964) developed a different image, emphasizing how aridity was an important environmental constraint that sharply distinguished the West from the East. However, Webb argued that it was the technology of the industrialized East—windmills, barbed wire, and

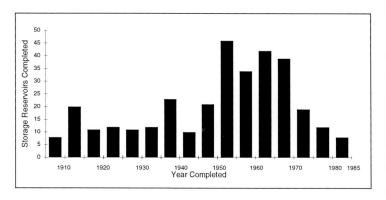

FIGURE 1.4 Dam-building efforts were relatively steady through 1950 but more than doubled in the two decades following World War II. In 1993, the Commissioner of Reclamation confirmed the downward trend of the past two decades when he announced that the dam-building era had ended and the Bureau of Reclamation would not be planning any new reservoirs. (Adapted from U.S. Bureau of Reclamation 1986)

six-shooters—that made it possible for Easterners to exploit the rich natural resources of the West in an essentially colonial relationship.

The third and still developing historical paradigm of "new Western history" emphasizes the similarities and continuities between the East and West, portraying the population of the West as being almost as urbanized, complex, and hierarchically structured as the East (e.g., Limerick, Milner, and Rankin 1991). This new paradigm suggests that much of the concentration of economic and political power stems from control of natural resources, such as water, and in fact, it has been argued that dam building has created a "hydraulic empire" in the West (Worster 1985). Adopting the perspective of "new social historians" of the 1960s and 1970s (e.g., Demos 1970) and the "new labor historians" (e.g., Fink 1990), the new historians of the West are especially cognizant of the viewpoint of ordinary and often overlooked people, that is, the "powerless, the inarticulate [and] the poor [who] have been treated no more fairly by historians than they have been treated by their contemporaries" (Lemisch 1969:29). Labor historians are no longer solely focusing on worker organizations and labor ideology but are examining "the experiences of working people in their private lives, work places, and communities" (Moody 1990:ix).

Anthropologists have long recognized that a bottom-up perspective of a culture can be just as enlightening as top-down histories of famous leaders or unique events. Historical archaeology today is practiced primarily as a subdiscipline of anthropology, and historical archaeologists commonly investigate the remains left by ordinary people (e.g., Ascher 1974; Deetz 1977; Gradwohl and Osborn 1984). This has not always been so. Recent reviews identified five overlapping traditions within historical archaeology, and much of the early research focused on restoration of famous historical locales such as Jamestown, Virginia, and West Point's Fort Putnam (Gruber 1984; Teague 1987, 1988).

As historical archaeology developed in the borderland between history and anthropology, there was considerable jousting among those arguing for primacy of either written documents—the traditional source material of history—or artifacts and physical remains—the domain of archaeology (e.g., Cleland and Fitting 1968; Dollar 1968; Fontana 1968; Harrington 1955; Noel Hume 1961, 1975). Fortunately, such turf battling gave way to general recognition that historical archaeology prospers by combining the strengths of both the historical and anthropological disciplines.

The maturing field of historical archaeology now routinely uses both historical and archaeological evidence to produce a fuller understanding of the past than either history or archaeology alone would permit. Some events leave few material clues for archaeological study—a fatal accident involving a drowning at a reservoir, for example. However, the same event might be writ large in historical documents such as newspapers, diaries, or insurance files. Historical sources may also reveal a person's thoughts, motives, and feelings—intangibles that archaeologists can only infer.

Archaeology, on the other hand, has two main strengths compared with historical records. Some objects are so mundane, so commonplace, that they are nearly invisible to writers. What diarist or reporter describes a man's shoes in detail, or a child's broken toy, or how a can of beans is sealed? Yet clothes, toys, and cans may become archaeological relics and provide clues to reconstruct how everyday lives felt, looked, and smelled.

Archaeology's other strength is the stuff of new Western history. Unlike many historical documents, the archaeological record is not biased in its treatment of ordinary people and minorities. At least in this regard, archaeological artifacts do not lie. In the written historical record, the Apaches of Roosevelt are nearly invisible, but they left a wealth of artifacts scattered on the ground for the skilled archaeologist to read. James Deetz (1988:363), a pioneer among historical archaeologists, says that "archeology's prime value to history lies in its promise to take into account large numbers of people in the past who were either not included in the written record, or if they were, were included in either a biased or minimal way."

Thus, historical archaeology is a natural ally of the new Western history. In fact, Limerick (1993) suggests that writer Wallace Stegner, who first broached many of the research themes of new Western history, anticipated the value of historic archaeology when as a boy more than half a century ago, he rummaged around his local town dump in Whitemud, Saskatchewan. Stegner came to realize that mundane trash may be the only source of local cultural history and that such an artifactual record is an unbiased record of ordinary lives—not an edited selection of only the "prettified" aspects of our history.

In sum, we used historical archaeology as a tool for seeking a bottom-up view of life in the construction camps where the people who built the dams of central Arizona lived. We used historical archaeology to learn something about the men whose calloused hands dug the earth, placed the stones, mixed the concrete, and strung the power lines. We used historical archaeology to reveal the grit and smell, the taste and texture, and the danger and discrimination that were part of the lives of the people who raised these dams. In a real sense, the hands of such laborers built the West we inhabit. Blending history and archaeology, we hoped to recover a sense of what life and work were like for some of our predecessors in the Arizona desert and, at the same time, gain an appreciation of the processes that influenced their lives and still affect ours.

Our study of dam construction camps was by no means the first historical archaeology project to focus on temporary communities of laborers. To mention just a few examples, many short-lived mining communities have been investigated, including several in Arizona, such as the Jackrabbit, Reward, and Rosemont mines (Ayres 1984; Reynolds and others 1974; Teague 1980). The camps of railroad construction workers are another type of temporary laborer community that has been studied in many states of the West, including Idaho, Utah, Colorado, Texas, and Arizona (Anderson 1983; Briggs 1974; Buckles 1976; Rossillon 1984; Stone and Fedick 1990; Wegars and Sprague 1981). A few archaeological sites related to water-resource development have also been recorded, such as the construction camp at Elephant Butte Dam in New Mexico (Boyd and Etchieson 1986) and camps along the Los Angeles Aqueduct (Costello and Marvin 1992). These archaeology studies are complemented by social histories such as Stevens' (1988) history of the construction of Hoover Dam, and the documentary film of the construction of Kerr Dam in Montana (Bigcrane and Smith 1991).

Nevertheless, the historical archaeology of temporary laborer camps is still at a nascent stage of development. Research strategies, analytical methods, and conclusions vary from project to project. We pursued the investigation of dam construction camps in central Arizona as a case study that might eventually contribute to more meaningful comparisons and syntheses of these temporary communities in the West.

The historical archaeology of this project built upon earlier archaeological and historical research into the construction camp at the Granite Reef Diversion Dam (Brown 1978), the construction contractor's camp at Roosevelt Dam (Hantman and McKenna 1985), and the power canal at Roosevelt (Ayres 1983). Our studies were on a much larger scale than these three earlier investigations and involved several research historians and a crew of approximately a dozen archaeologists. Field crews worked full-time for almost a year, from July 1986 into May 1987, studying fifty-eight archaeological sites (see "The Daily Life of an Archaeologist," p. 26).

Not all, but most of the sites were related to historic dam construction camps at the seven major irrigation storage dams in central Arizona. Because most of the camps were occupied more than once, either to finish work left undone or to modify the original dams, the site inventories had the potential to reflect almost twenty temporary construction camps spanning a half century of dam building (fig 1.5).

The field archaeologists found the quality of the archaeological record to be better at some sites than others, with the best information being recovered near the Roosevelt and Waddell dams. The more than one thousand archaeological features defined during the course of fieldwork primarily reflect the former locations of temporary housing, including tent houses, simple frame buildings, and *wickiups* (traditional Apache houses), as well as a few public buildings such as mess halls, industrial facilities such as cableway platforms and powderhouses, piles of trash, and remnants of utilities such as water, sewer, and electrical systems.

Artifacts were collected from thirty-nine of the sites, totaling almost 144,000 items estimated to represent a minimum of more than 83,000 whole and fragmentary artifacts and faunal specimens. The collections are dominated by nails, tin cans,

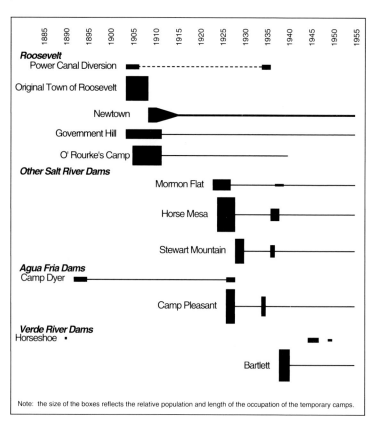

FIGURE 1.5 Construction camps were investigated at seven dam locales. Because many of the camps were reoccupied to complete work left unfinished or to modify the original dams, almost twenty temporary dam construction communities formed and disbanded in central Arizona between 1890 and 1950. (Courtesy of Dames & Moore)

and broken glass and ceramics. Months and months of laboratory efforts were required to identify the collections and to build computerized files of information.

In addition to the archaeologists working in the field and laboratory, the research team included a cultural anthropologist, a sociologist, and several historians. Writing the social history of ordinary people who produced few written documents requires identification and review of nontraditional source materials such as manuscript census records, court documents, agency files, project archives, contemporary newspapers, periodicals, and trade journals, as well as compilation of oral histories through interviews (see "Boxes in the Basement: A Historian's Day at Work," p. 28). The resulting reconstruction of daily life in the historic dam construction camps of central Arizona is a multifaceted compilation from disparate lines of evidence and perspectives. The chapters that follow attempt to convey this diversity and provide a sense of what it was like to live in those temporary construction communities. The research focused on four themes in the construction camps: (1) demography of the camps, (2) daily life, (3) the nature of work, and (4) ethnic relations.

The central Arizona dams are monuments to what temporary laboring communities were able to achieve. Because the dams are fully functioning and integral parts of the water supply system that still serves the Salt River Valley, they have an obvious and monumental, but perhaps not fully appreciated, relevance for our modern lives. Beyond that significance, the story of life in the dam construction camps provides a useful perspective on our current transient, multicultural lives in the American West, lives that have more parallels with the temporary historic construction camps than might be anticipated.

Although he is often credited as the first Anglo to envision irrigation in the Salt River Valley, John W. "Jack" Swilling (fig. 1.6) was only one of several people who recognized the potential usefulness of the routes and remnants of prehistoric irrigation canals. The first water claims on the Salt River anticipated Swilling's claims by half a year, and the siting of the original town of Phoenix bypassed Swilling's settlement.

Anglo settlers had come to the valley as early as 1865, when Camp McDowell was established to control the Apaches and Yavapais. At first, the settlers simply harvested the lush native grasses that grew along the river banks. In 1866, Camillo C. C. Carr, an army officer, began to divert the water of the Salt River into ditches, watering newly planted fields and often reopening segments of prehistoric Hohokam canals. Four miners filed the first formal water rights claim on the Salt River in June 1867, followed the next day by the claim filed by Carr and three other army officers.

Both groups claimed water for the north bank of the river at Maryville, the first Anglo settlement in the valley. The settlement grew where two primitive wagon roads, the Camp McDowell–Maricopa Wells road and the Wickenburg road, met and crossed the river at the Salt River Crossing, sometimes called the Maricopa Crossing. An article in the *Arizona Miner* described the crops growing at Maryville in July 1867 as "promising [with] large yields expected."

Jack Swilling's entrepreneurial mind may have been sparked by a visit to the hay camps near Maryville in the fall of 1867, but whatever the source of his inspiration, Swilling convinced Wickenburg investors to join him in forming the Swilling Irrigating and Canal Company in November of that year (Salt River Project History Museum 1992). The company completed an irrigation ditch by March 1868, several miles downstream from the Maryville community. By the next spring, three members of the company were cultivating three hundred acres of wheat, barley, corn, and sorghum; six other farmers cultivated a total of four hundred acres using Swilling Ditch water.

Swilling and his neighbors along the ditch called their community the Phoenix Settlement and expanded their farming interests across the valley. Over the five years from 1868 to 1873, Swilling excavated five additional canals branching off

the Salt River and built himself a large adobe home known as "Swilling's Castle."

Despite the castle, Swilling was unable to promote his Phoenix Settlement as the central place of the Salt River Valley. His community lost both the permanent Phoenix town site and the Maricopa County seat to a newer community farther downstream. Swilling sold his holdings and moved north to the Black Canyon area in 1873.

The causes of significant historical events tend to be multifaceted. From our perspective, the initiation of a new era of irrigation in the Salt River Valley is a counterexample to the "great man" theory of history. It was not the genius of Swilling, or Carr, or any of the other miners or soldiers that spawned a new age of irrigation. Swilling's name probably is remembered not because he was among the first to dig a canal along the route of a prehistoric Hohokam canal, but because of his flamboyant life and ignominious death in prison after he was accused of robbing the Wickenburg stagecoach.

With or without Swilling's personality and insight, or that of any of the other early irrigators, it seems inevitable that the forces driving American settlement of the Southwest would have resulted in a new era of irrigation agriculture by the end of the 1860s. It was a development being driven by a variety of factors, and simply attributing it to the insight of Swilling, or any other individual, begs a more complete understanding of these historical processes.

The variability of the Southwest's climate becomes more obvious with each additional year of weather records. Good records have been kept in central Arizona for less than a century and were almost nonexistent when Roosevelt Dam was designed as the first major water storage dam in Arizona. A crucial step in the design process is determining the magnitude of river flows so that spillways can be sized sufficiently large to safely pass floods without overtopping the dam. Water flowing over the top of a dam can quickly erode it, leading to catastrophic failure, such as happened at Walnut Creek Dam on the Hassayampa River in 1890 (Dill 1987). Precipitation records compiled since the completion of Roosevelt Dam and the lower dams on the Salt River have led hydrologists to rethink the magnitude of floods that can be expected. This is why Roosevelt Dam is being raised by more than seventy feet.

Climatologists have come to appreciate a statistical paradox. They have detected little evidence that the average climate of the Southwest has changed or is changing significantly, but they have come to realize that it is normal to expect huge variations above or below the averages in any given year. A recent study extended historical climate records back into prehistory by analyzing the varying widths of tree rings in the Salt and Verde watersheds to reconstruct the annual flows in the Salt River through central Arizona during the years A.D. 740 to 1370 (Nials, Gregory, and Graybill 1989). The study demonstrated that the average summer flows have been remarkably stable over this 630-year period, but winter patterns were even more variable than historic records document. Only about half of the annual flows could be considered close to the average of about 900,000 acre-feet per year. This means that unusually dry years, or much wetter than normal years, are common.

The greatest reconstructed flow occurred in the year A.D. 899, when it is estimated that more than 2.5 million acre-feet of water ran through the Salt River (fig. 1.7). The runoff, enough to fill Lake Roosevelt twice, would have been much greater than any recorded during the historic era. Even in a desert, too much rain is as bad as too little, and the resulting 630-year flood of A.D. 899 certainly would have devastated the Hohokam irrigation system. Decades ago, archaeologists defined a major change in the Hohokam culture and labeled it as the transition between the Colonial and Sedentary periods. Interestingly, they

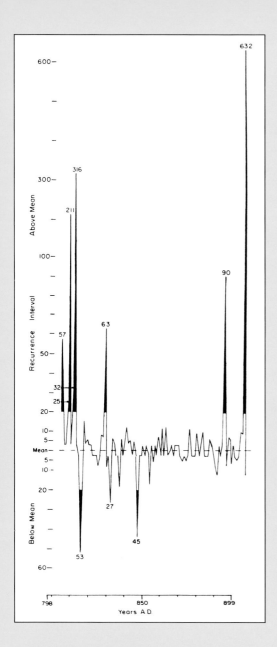

FIGURE 1.7 These estimated stream flows for A.D. 798–899 are based on variations in the width of tree rings in the upper watershed of the Salt River drainage. The reconstructions document a couple of major droughts and a half dozen major floods during the ninth century. (Adapted from Nials, Gregory, and Graybill 1989:65)

dated this change to about A.D. 900, and it seems likely that the great flood of A.D. 899 was causally related to these cultural changes.

Nevertheless, the Hohokam rebuilt their canals, their population grew, and their cultural system became more complex than before the great flood of A.D. 899. There is no indication in the archaeological record that the Hohokam did not feel secure in their way of life before it collapsed quite suddenly—at least from an archaeological perspective—approximately a century before the first Spanish explorers arrived in 1539.

To what levels of rainfall should cultures in desert environments adapt? By building storage dams and mining groundwater, our culture has chosen to rely on a much larger supply of annual water than did the prehistoric Hohokam (Bowden 1977). As a result, our population is much larger, and our lifeway more complex, than the Hohokam ever imagined. Could a string of not average but *normal* dry years or another *630-year flood* be disastrous for the complex system we have built in the Sonoran Desert?

POWER FOR SCIENCE: JOHN WESLEY POWELL

Systems analysts have often documented how seemingly insignificant events can trigger chain reactions that result in unforeseen outcomes as systems evolve. From our perspective, the life of John Wesley Powell (1834–1902) (fig. 1.8) triggered divergent events that have once again converged in our studies of historic construction camps at Roosevelt Dam.

Powell is often remembered as the first person to successfully raft and map the Colorado River through the Grand Canyon, but he should be remembered for much more (Stegner 1954). Having lost an arm as a Civil War hero, Major Powell went on to direct one of the four great post–Civil War surveys of the West (Goetzmann 1966). These surveys led to the creation of the U.S. Geological Survey in 1879, and Powell served as the agency's second director from 1881 to 1894. In this position, he became the premier government scientist of his time. He also won congressional authorization to undertake an irrigation survey of the West—a study that eventually led to the creation of the U.S. Reclamation Service, which in turn led to the construction of Roosevelt Dam.

From 1879 to 1902, Powell also served as the first director of the Bureau of American Ethnology (BAE), which gave him the opportunity to pursue the interests he had developed in American Indian cultures during the course of his surveys of the West (Judd 1967). Under Powell's guidance, the BAE became the country's leading anthropological research institution at a time when the discipline was first accepted as a legitimate academic pursuit, which in turn nurtured the subdiscipline of archaeology. Thus the archaeological investigation of the historic construction camps at Roosevelt, as well as the dam itself, is the result of Powell's influence.

FIGURE 1.8 John Hillers took this photograph of John Wesley Powell on the Kaibab Plateau near the Grand Canyon during the Powell Expedition of 1871–1875. Through such experiences, Powell learned much about the Southwestern environment and the native peoples who had adapted to its rigors. (Courtesy of the Smithsonian Institution National Anthropological Archives, Bureau of American Ethnology Collection)

Despite his long legacy, Powell's involvement in the irrigation movement was a personal disappointment. The authorization for the irrigation study gave him the prerogative to suspend homesteading of the lands he was investigating, and his studies led him to argue that careful planning would be needed to develop environmentally sound approaches for settling the West. However, this was seen as too much power for science over free enterprise, and the laissez-faire political forces that favored continued, immediate homesteading won the day (Dupree 1957). Powell was forced to resign his directorship of the Geological Survey, and he retreated to the BAE, where he worked until his death in 1902. Paradoxically, that was the year the Reclamation Service was established and the American Anthropological Association (AAA) was founded. The AAA played a key role in formulating the Antiquities Act that Congress passed in 1906 (Lee 1970), the first federal historic preservation legislation and the forerunner of the current policies that led to our studies.

THE SYMBOLISM OF WATERING THE WEST

Twenty-seven-year-old William Ellsworth Smythe left his New England home in 1888 to pursue a journalism career in Nebraska (Worster 1985). Soon after his arrival, he witnessed the effects of a disastrous drought and became a convert to the reclamation movement, as the effort to promote irrigation agriculture in the West was called. Smythe went on to become the leading zealot of the irrigation crusade. He founded the Irrigation Congress and initiated publication of a journal, *The Irrigation Age*, in 1891 (Malone and Etulain 1989).

Smythe believed that the aridity of the West was part of a grand providential plan to challenge and reform America (Limerick 1987). He vehemently argued that it was the government's duty to assist in developing irrigation systems in the West in order to create opportunities for some of the middle class in the East, who were being squeezed by big business as well as the burgeoning flow of immigrants. Smythe's vision of the West was not a simple re-creation of a Jeffersonian agrarian economy based on small independent farms, but he did believe that small farms organized on the model of joint-stock companies could be developed throughout the West to bring the region into the industrial age (Worster 1985).

The Irrigation Congress that Smythe founded held its first international meeting in 1891 in Salt Lake City—an appropriate setting because Mormon settlement served as a model for cooperative development of irrigation systems. Two years later in Los Angeles, at the second meeting of the Irrigation Congress, John Wesley Powell was hooted from the speaker's platform when he dared to point out that the West's water supply was simply too meager to ever farm more than about a tenth of the land. Smythe, the zealot, won out over the scientific facts and figures of the "technobureaucrats."

The figure of a woman pouring water from an urn came to be a common symbol of the irrigation crusade, and it was used on mastheads and meeting programs. Archaeologists recovered a delegate badge with this symbol from the burned remains of a *wickiup* (traditional house) at one of the Apache laborer camps at Roosevelt (fig. 1.9). The ritually "killed" pots and pans from this part of the camp indicate that the wickiup was very likely burned as part of a mortuary ceremony when one of the residents died. The badge had been carefully cut in half, and only part of it was found. The female figure on the badge is pouring water onto a map of New Mexico, suggesting the medallion was struck for the sixteenth Irrigation Congress held in Albuquerque in 1908 (fig. 1.10). We can guess that some engineer associated with the Roosevelt Dam project attended the convention, but why the badge was cut in two, how it came to be deposited

FIGURE 1.9 (upper right)
This image of a woman
pouring water on the
desert was a common
symbol used by promoters
of the irrigation and
reclamation movement,
championing the use of
technology to overcome
environmental challenges.
This artifact, recovered
from an Apache camp at
Roosevelt, appears to be
half of a badge worn by a
delegate to an irrigation or
reclamation congress,
probably the Sixteenth
National Irrigation
Congress held in
Albuquerque in 1908.
Why the badge was cut in
two and how it came to be
deposited in an Apache
camp remains a mystery.
(Courtesy of Dames &
Moore)

FIGURE 1.10 (lower left)
In addition to this image
of science bidding the
desert to drink,
proponents of the
irrigation movement used
slogans such as "save the
forests," "store the floods,"
"reclaim the deserts," and
"make homes on the
land." (From the program
of the Sixteenth National
Irrigation Congress, Albuquerque, New Mexico,
1908)

in an Apache laborer camp, and what the woman pouring water symbolized for its Apache owner is far from clear.

We do know that some artifacts were religious symbols for Apaches. From about 1903 to 1907, a cross and crescent symbol was adopted by followers of a messianic cult known as *Daagodighá*. One historical photograph of an Apache man at Roosevelt shows this symbol cut from a piece of metal and attached to his watch fob. A second photograph shows the symbol made from a piece of ribbon and worn on the shirt of an Apache laborer.

These photographs suggest that some of the Apaches at Roosevelt were believers in *Daagodighá*, which means "they will be raised up" (Ferg 1987:144). Those who wore the symbol and marked their property with it were to be lifted into the sky at the appointed time when the earth would be purged of evil by a flood or earthquake. Believers could then return to live in a rejuvenated world of peace and plenty.

Such messianic cults or revitalization movements spread among American Indian groups in response to the suffering and oppression they endured as they were conquered. The most famous of these movements, known by Euro-Americans as the Ghost Dance, originated among the Paiutes of Nevada around 1870 (Mooney 1965). The leader of this movement preached that divine intervention would eliminate the white men and restore Indian societies to their aboriginal way of life.

It may be easy to dismiss such messianic cults as dated, lamentable aberrations spawned by cultures in conflict, and to cast the forlorn longing for a better life as understandable, but unrealistic, nostalgia. The image of a woman pouring water on the deserts of the West to make them bloom is also a dated symbol, but in many ways the reclamation movement it represents is a messianic cult whose followers believe technology can be used to create a paradise. The cult persists largely unquestioned, but its long-term viability remains to be tested.

THE DAILY LIFE OF AN ARCHAEOLOGIST

Thanks to the Indiana Jones movies, archaeologists are popularly imagined to be dashing professors in tweed jackets, who lecture captivated students about their adventures in exotic lands. Sometimes they are imagined as being called from their classrooms to take urgent messages from foreign diplomats who need help saving invaluable antiquities. Within a matter of days, the archaeologists have traveled halfway around the globe and faced death, destruction, and inevitably romance before returning as heroes after saving a precious treasure from destruction.

In reality, however, the lives of archaeologists are much more mundane (fig. 1.11). Today, most archaeological research in the United States is undertaken under the rubric of *cultural resource management* (Rogge 1983). Historic preservation laws have been steadily strengthened since the mid-1960s, enabling archaeologists to review most public projects for potential effects on archaeological resources. This was the stimulus for the present study.

Sizeable armies of archaeologists are now employed to walk rights-of-way for new highways, pipelines, mines, and timber sales. It is labor-intensive work because they are commonly required to walk no farther than fifty feet apart as they cover vast acreages. The work is often in remote locations and some-

FIGURE 1.11 Archaeology crew members Ron Savage and Noreen Fritz work at a plane table to get the details right for an archaeological map of the Camp Pleasant site. (Courtesy of Dames & Moore)

times requires camping out or staying in motels in out-of-the-way places rarely visited by the average traveler. These archaeologists tend to be bright and well educated but poorly paid in consideration of their credentials. Many live from one contract study to the next, without ever being offered a permanent job with fringe benefits. They might be surveying a gas pipeline in Wyoming during hot, windswept days one summer, and plunging through tick-infested wetlands in Louisiana examining land for a new highway during the next season.

The valiant crew members who participated in the crucial work of collecting field data for our study of the historic dam construction camps of central Arizona had the experience of enduring summer heat of up to 110°F while keeping a wary eye out for rattlesnakes, and then, a few months later, trying to warm numb fingers while screening soil for artifacts. The crew incorporated archaeologists from many different parts of the country who came together to work towards a common goal. Once the work was done, they moved on to the next project. In many ways, these transient archaeologists are modern society's closest analog to the historic construction workers. The crew of archaeologists who worked on the project acquired an understanding of what day-to-day life was like in the historic construction camps not simply because they recovered archaeological information, but also because they lived lives that were in some ways reminiscent of the lives of transient historic laborers.

Although many major historical events have been researched, analyzed, and written about in easily accessible publications, much of the raw material for as-yet-unwritten histories lies forgotten in storerooms. Historians often have to "dig" for buried information much as archaeologists do, particularly when attempting to write the social history of ordinary people.

The search for relevant records of the historic dam construction camps of central Arizona began at the Department of Library, Archives, and Public Records at the state capitol in Phoenix, the central repository for Arizona state and county public records. After examining the Phoenix newspapers archived there, the researchers were stymied by the lack of public records from the Roosevelt Dam construction era. Concluding that the records probably had never been transferred from Gila County, the historian sleuths left the air-conditioned order of the state archives and traveled to Globe, the county seat.

They found only more frustration at the Gila County Courthouse: not one of the clerks knew of any public records from the dam construction era. After they had questioned at least a dozen friendly but unhelpful people, a woman who was a member of the Gila County Historical Society suggested that it might be worth investigating the *old* county courthouse (fig. 1.12), which had been built in 1906 by Peter Wilson, a stone masonry subcontractor on the Roosevelt Dam project (Bigando 1989).

The historians arrived at the old courthouse to find a crew of carpenters and painters busy adapting the building for reuse as an art museum, but they decided to push on, despite the inappropriateness of their business attire. Stepping over and around the construction debris, they headed for the basement and a vault-like door at the bottom of the stairs.

Behind the door, they found a musty storeroom filled with boxes, files, stacks of papers, and tax books. Beyond the first room was a maze of smaller storerooms stuffed with masses of records. The inch-thick layer of dust was a sure sign that no one had disturbed the storage area for decades, nor had the records ever been catalogued or filed in any sort of order.

Random opening of boxes revealed documents ranging from 1920s gasoline receipts to earlier naturalization records. On a whim, one of the historians climbed a stepladder to retrieve a

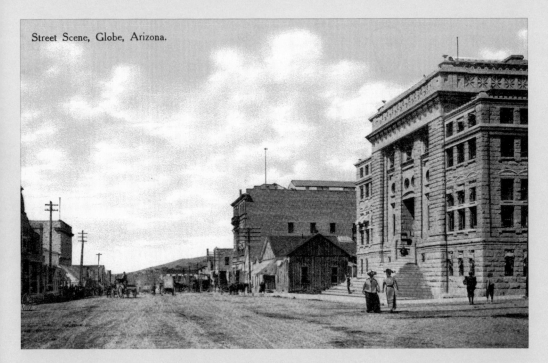
Street Scene, Globe, Arizona.

box stored on a high shelf and found the equivalent of an archaeologist's trove of golden treasure: school records from the Roosevelt area during the time of the dam construction. These handwritten student rosters revealed fascinating information on population, families, and ethnicity of the ordinary people in the Roosevelt dam construction community.

Although the historians continued digging into the boxes in the basement for several days, they never found anything to top that first day's find of school records. The state archivist was informed about the treasure of documents buried in the old Gila County Courthouse basement, but given the limitations of state funds, it is likely that the dusty boxes of records will remain in Globe, undisturbed, until they are rediscovered by some future historian.

FIGURE 1.12 Historic records were found in the basement of the former Gila County Courthouse (far right), which was built in 1907 during the time Roosevelt Dam was being constructed. Local historic preservation efforts have succeeded in adapting the building for reuse as a community center. (Courtesy of Melissa Keane)

2

Daily Life

The desert that surrounds Lake Roosevelt is a challenging place to survive without today's air-conditioned technology. Vistas are impressive, but much of the land is rocky, and the sparse ground cover is prickly. Summer temperatures often top 100°F. Rainfall may be scarce for months at a time. Yet for thousands of years, people have lived in and roamed the desert canyons and valley floors of the Tonto Basin.

The most impressive archaeological sites found in the Tonto Basin are remnants of the prehistoric Salado, including the cliff dwellings that have been preserved as the Tonto National Monument. Like the Hohokam, their cousins in the Phoenix Basin, the Salado built and inhabited large, sprawling towns on the valley floor. Recent archaeological research has demonstrated that these prehistoric towns were complexes of apartments and granaries. Some had ceremonial buildings erected on artificial mounds surrounded by massive walls. The Salado irrigated, although not as extensively as the Hohokam, and grew corn, cotton, and other crops. For reasons that remain obscure but which probably relate to the roughly concurrent demise of the Hohokam, the civilization of the Salado farmers collapsed about A.D. 1450.

About a century after the Salado disappeared, and just as the first Spanish explorers probed Arizona, Apaches moved into the Tonto Basin, apparently from New Mexico. The highly mobile

In the American West we live surrounded by a wondrous, complex, often atrocious history. It's a story we need to make sense of, emotionally and morally, if we are ever to understand ourselves. But, as is commonplace to say, the past is a foreign country. We have to live there a while, emotionally, in our imaginations, speaking the language and eating the food, in touch with the people, before we can hope to see ourselves truly. History is something that happened to people like ourselves, and it is happening to us.

—WILLIAM KITTREDGE (1987:84)

nomads obtained horses from the Spanish, and their impermanent camps and dwellings left few traces in the archaeological
record. Throughout Arizona's period of Mexican rule, through
the early years of United States control, through the Civil War
and into the 1870s, the fiercely independent Apaches waged
spirited battles against those who moved into their lands. The
Apaches of the Tonto Basin fought to keep their homeland free
of settlers until the late 1870s, when the U.S. Army forced most
of them onto reservations.

In the last decades of the nineteenth century, ranchers settled in the Tonto Basin, and prospectors sought precious metals
in the surrounding hills and canyons. These people left the first
significant marks on the land since the prehistoric Salado, yet
their fences, corrals, stables, ranch houses, trails, mine shafts,
and tailing piles would soon be overshadowed by the great
dams of the early twentieth century.

When the U.S. Reclamation Service was created in 1902, it
was charged with financing, designing, and building water
projects to spur development in the arid West. Entrepreneurs
and visionaries in Arizona had vigorously lobbied Congress in
support of the new agency, and they were eager to take advantage of its mandate. One of the first projects approved by the
Reclamation Service was a dam across the Salt River where it
exited the Tonto Basin.

Roosevelt's Boom Town History

As early as 1889, the narrow canyon below the confluence of
the Salt River and Tonto Creek had been identified as a promising dam site, and in 1902, federal surveyors came to make
topographic maps. By 1903, the dam builders set out in earnest
first to build Roosevelt Dam, then others, to impound the waters of the Salt River to irrigate downstream fields and to generate electricity for the expanding mines, farms, and population
centers of central Arizona.

Damming the Salt River in this inaccessible spot was a monumental task. The dam site, sixty miles east of Phoenix, was
linked to the capital city of some six thousand people only by
primitive trails through the Salt River Canyon. The site was
more closely connected to Globe, a mining town of a few thousand residents located twenty-five miles southeast of the dam
site. Although only eighty miles apart, the towns of Phoenix
and Globe were linked by convoluted railroad connections of
more than three hundred miles.

Raising the 250-foot-high Roosevelt Dam was only half of the job tackled by project engineers and laborers. The other half of the $10 million project involved support facilities: a diversion dam and 19-mile power canal brought water to the dam site to generate hydroelectric power during construction; a cement plant and associated quarries provided limestone, sand, and clay; other quarries provided the great stone blocks for the masonry dam itself; logging camps and sawmills in the Sierra Ancha Mountains to the east of the Tonto Basin supplied lumber; telephone lines and improved roads connected the dam site to Globe and Phoenix; and the Apache Trail brought supplies and tourists from Mesa and Phoenix through the rugged canyon of the Salt River to the dam. Work on these ancillary but necessary facilities began in 1903, and three years passed before workers were able to lay the first stone block for the dam itself.

Boom town communities appeared during the long construction period, but they disappeared when the work was finished. In the early years, from 1903 to 1905, Reclamation Service engineers and office personnel lived at Livingston (fig. 2.1). The small ranching settlement, some eight miles upstream of the Roosevelt Dam site, was close to the dam that had to be built first to divert water into the power canal. Construction of this canal across the rugged terrain proved to be the first of many unforeseen challenges for the Reclamation Service. The agency engineers responded by developing state-of-the-art technology in the remote Arizona Territory, including a "concrete alligator" to pour jointless concrete pipes for inverted siphons to carry the power canal beneath Pinto, Schoolhouse, and Cottonwood creeks (Introcaso 1984).

The final cost of the power canal was tenfold the original estimate as it neared completion in 1905, and the focus of the construction work shifted downstream to the main dam. Government personnel moved downstream and, with newly hired laborers, established communities much closer to the dam site (figs. 2.2 and 2.3). The men who built Roosevelt Dam worked either directly for the Reclamation Service or for John O'Rourke and Company, the Texas contractor who won the contract to build the dam itself.

To accommodate the dozens of engineers and hundreds of workers employed to build the dam, Globe and Salt River Valley businessmen opened commercial enterprises at the government town site on the first rise south of the Salt River, three-quarters of a mile upstream of the dam site. Commercial lots

FIGURE 2.1 On February 7, 1904, Roosevelt engineers, laborers, and their wives lined up their horses for a group photograph. The tent houses of Livingston, the first headquarters camp for the Reclamation Service, can be seen in the background. (Courtesy of the Salt River Project)

were leased by the government to business owners at no rental, but there were restrictions, the most significant being the prohibition of liquor within a three-mile radius of any Reclamation Service operation or work camp (*Arizona Republican* [AR] 26 June 1904). By January 1904, Roosevelt, as the town was called, had a postmaster, three general stores, a drug store, a private doctor, and a government doctor. It also boasted a barber shop, a shoe shop, a livery stable, a meat market, two restaurants, and two lodging houses (AR 31 Jan 1904). By spring, the town had acquired a fourth general store and a second pair of restaurants, as well as about sixty tents and a dozen frame buildings for housing. A *Saturday Review* (April 1904) article described Roosevelt as a "live, up-to-date little town with electric lights." The town soon featured a pavilion for Saturday night dances, and twenty-five-cent ice cream sodas flowed from the fountain of druggist Warren Barnett (AR 26 June 1904).

The boom town of Roosevelt, in many ways, fit the popular image of frontier Western towns. Simple board-and-batten, one- and two-story buildings were arranged along both sides of a single, wide dirt street, and a sprinkling wagon helped to keep the dust down (AR 26 June 1904). Some tent structures were interspersed among the wooden buildings with their shingled gable roofs, deep overhanging porches, and wooden sidewalks (figs. 2.4, 2.5, and 2.6). Many workers lived in tents, tent houses, and adobe structures haphazardly arranged on the outskirts of town, a five-minute walk from any of the businesses in Roosevelt. Apache laborers and their families lived in traditional wickiups in separate camps near Roosevelt (see "Photographs of Daily Life," p. 72).

FIGURE 2.2 In this panorama of the Roosevelt settlements taken in January 1907, Government Hill is to the left, the cement mill is on the hill in the center, and the settlement of Roosevelt sprawls across the first rise above the Salt River. O'Rourke's Camp is on the hill slope on the right. The site of Roosevelt Dam is in the cleft between O'Rourke's Camp and the cement mill. (Courtesy of the Arizona State Archives, *Dam Projects: Box 1, File 13; Arizona State Archives, Department of Library, Archives and Public Records*)

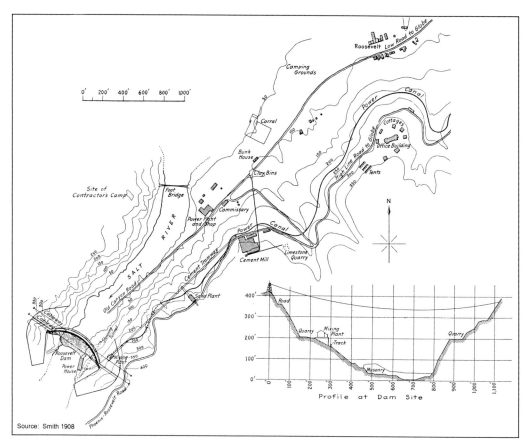

FIGURE 2.3 The town of old Roosevelt and O'Rourke's Camp ("Site of Contractor's Camp") are shown on this map prepared for an article published by Chester Smith in *Engineering News* (60:266). "Office Building," "Tents" (Bullpen), and "Cottages" mark the location of Government Hill. The profile conveys a sense of the dramatic and dangerous topography at the dam site.

In June 1904, work began on an office building and housing for the Reclamation Service staff at the best location near the dam site, the point of a ridge some 350 feet above the Salt River and the town of Roosevelt. Government Hill, or Roosevelt-on-the-Hill as it was sometimes called, was largely completed by May 1905 and housed government employees from chief engineer Louis Hill to the Chinese cook, Ah Soo. Some worked on Government Hill, and some walked downhill to the power canal, the cement mill, and the dam itself.

The orderly, well-built community on Government Hill featured a headquarters building for the Reclamation Service, a large dining hall and kitchen, an ice plant, a hospital or clinic, and even a tennis court. Senior engineers and their families lived in comfortably furnished frame cottages equipped with electricity, indoor plumbing, and porcelain bathtubs. Junior bachelor engineers lived in tent houses on the western slopes of Government Hill in an area known as "the Bullpen" (Palmer 1979). Residents of the Hill enjoyed a magnificent view of the Salt River and the Tonto Basin, and, as the reservoir filled, of Lake Roosevelt (figs. 2.7, 2.8, 2.9, 2.10, and 2.11).

A third community emerged in the Roosevelt area in 1905, when construction contractor John O'Rourke planned and built a community to house his employees (fig. 2.12). O'Rourke's Camp, on the north side of the Salt River adjacent to the dam site, included only a few wood-frame buildings. Most of the construction engineers, foremen, stonecutters, masons, derrick operators, and unskilled laborers lived in a cluster of about fifty tent houses. Many engineers and their families lived and ate in a sixteen-room boardinghouse, while construction foremen lived in semiprivate tents. Workmen lived in larger tent bunk-houses.

O'Rourke also put up a house and office for himself, as well as a school, a recreation hall, a mercantile store, a commissary, corrals, a tack shop, and an ice house. Utilities were provided by telephone, water, and electrical lines, and a three-hundred-foot suspension bridge across the Salt River connected O'Rourke's Camp to Roosevelt and Government Hill on the south side of the river. Praise for the amenities of the newest Roosevelt community appeared in the April 19, 1906, *Arizona Republican*: "The camp is one of the most model in existence, Mr. O'Rourke evidently appreciating that in order to keep good men he must give them good accommodations. The men's quarters have cement floors, so that they can be easily and thoroughly cleaned, and iron beds and wire mattresses are used. In the camp is a complete ice plant and full paraphernalia for a model town." As engineers and laborers came to work on the dam project, the population of the camp grew from an initial contingent of about thirty to more than four hundred (Hantman and McKenna 1985; Smith 1912).

Despite the isolation and the summer heat of the Tonto Basin, O'Rourke's Camp and the other communities of Roosevelt grew into bustling settlements. Some local ranchers, after losing their lands to the new reservoir, went to work on the dam (Salt River Project Archives 1904–1911). Other local ranchers and businessmen took advantage of the financial opportunities provided by dam construction and supplied meat and other goods to the incoming workers and their families.

FIGURE 2.4 (overleaf) The Pioneer Restaurant and M. C. Webb & Sons Merchandise are at the far left, on the west end of the main street in old Roosevelt, November 1907. The building closest to the river has a "Laundry" sign above it. (Photograph by Walter Lubken, courtesy of the National Archives)

FIGURE 2.5 Roosevelt sported several restaurants to feed the workers, including a Mexican restaurant and this self-styled French establishment. (Courtesy of the Salt River Project)

Probably more than two thousand people were living in the Roosevelt area by 1907. In addition to those living in O'Rourke's Camp, on Government Hill, and in the town of Roosevelt, others lived outside these communities along the rural roads and on the scattered farms and ranches of the Tonto Basin. In addition, hundreds of American Indians, mostly Apaches, lived in camps along the river, on hillsides, along the power canal, near the diversion dam, and along the roads toward Globe.

Although the wood-frame buildings and tents of O'Rourke's Camp and Government Hill had been built high enough on the hillsides to be above water as the new lake filled, Roosevelt was less well sited. When heavy rains fell in 1908, and the reservoir began to fill behind the rising dam only five years after the first settlement of the town, Roosevelt residents haggled over a new location. Many of the merchants favored a move to the north side of the river, thinking it would be more accessible to local ranchers and prospectors, and to future tourists. However, the Reclamation Service preferred a site on the south side of the river, along the road to Globe and a mile upriver from Roosevelt, where Cottonwood Creek offered a ready supply of water.

In June 1908, the Reclamation Service surveyed the location for the new town and began to dismantle and move buildings.

In August, Roosevelt residents and merchants were told to begin moving their belongings, and by September, half of old Roosevelt had been moved uphill. "Sycamore," the name chosen by the Reclamation Service for the new location, did not take, and the local people referred to it as New Roosevelt or, more frequently, Newtown. By December, only the post office, the stage office, a few stores, and a barn and corral remained on the banks of the rising river.

Winter rains had already accelerated the rise of the river when, on December 13, a light rain began to fall. Three days later, the rain had grown heavier, but few residents were concerned about flooding until someone spotted a small cabin

FIGURE 2.6 Walter Lubken took this photograph in 1905 to document the government corral near Roosevelt, but note the tent house equipped with a sturdy masonry chimney at the far left. The corral and tent houses spread across the broad floodplain of the Salt River, visible in the background, were flooded when water began to back up behind the rising dam in late 1908. (Courtesy of the National Archives)

FIGURE 2.7 The U.S. Reclamation Service administration building dominates this circa 1906 photograph of Government Hill, but frame cottages and tent houses are also shown. The administration building is the only construction-era building on Government Hill that survives today. (Courtesy of the Salt River Project)

FIGURE 2.8 Tent houses built for bachelor engineers employed by the U.S. Reclamation Service clung to the hillsides of Government Hill. This cluster of tent houses was known to the residents as "the Bullpen." (Courtesy of the Salt River Project)

FIGURE 2.9 This photograph captures the "bachelor" ambience of one of the tent houses on Government Hill. Note the Christmas wreath, what might be a photograph of Mom back home in her garden, "pin-up" girls, and the reading material, which includes *Pearson's Magazines*, *Lost Lenore*, and *The American Monte Cristo*. (Courtesy of the National Archives)

FIGURE 2.10 The white-washed Reclamation Service dining hall on Government Hill offered white tablecloths, electric lights, and Worcestershire sauce. (January 1906, courtesy of the National Archives)

FIGURE 2.11 Cooks and cook's helpers posed for this 1905 photograph outside the large dining hall on Government Hill. (Courtesy of the Salt River Project)

floating down the river, which had rapidly become a lake. Workers rushed to the waterfront of old Roosevelt and hastily began to dismantle and move the remaining buildings and tents. With some "tall hustling," Postmaster Burtis, who had been caught up in a disagreement as to whether the post office should be moved to O'Rourke's Camp or Newtown, moved the contents of the post office to high ground just before the building itself floated off and was mired in mud about a hundred yards downstream (Zarbin 1984:190).

S. S. Thompson, a cement-mill worker and *Arizona Republican* correspondent, described the noises of that night and the sights of the next day.

It rained most of the night [December 16] and every once in a while the tent would whip loose from one corner of the building directly over our bed and relieve itself of all surplus water onto the bed covers. In the meantime, the lake was up to within four feet of our floor, and every time we woke up we would heave out a rock, with which we had

provided ourselves before retiring, to see if the water had
reached us yet. Providentially, the rise of the lake stopped
at about three feet before our level. . . . All night the crash
of adobe walls could be heard as the water reached them.
All night, also, could be heard at intervals the last cry of
some unfortunate cat which had found some wall as a
temporary place of safety, and succeeding the crash of the
wall would come the cry of the feline that had placed too
much faith on its stability and whose faith was rewarded
with a watery grave. . . . In the morning we found . . . over
a dozen houses were caught by the water and some of
them with all their belongings. . . . The church building
was flooded almost up to the eaves. . . . The waters of the
lake are backed up, both rivers out of sight, and this flood
ought to put a quietus on the croakers that have been laboring under the illusion that we never get enough rain in
Arizona . . . to fill the reservoir site at the Roosevelt Dam.
(AR 27 Dec 1908)

FIGURE 2.12 The waters of the new Lake Roosevelt are visible to the right in this photograph
taken on January 28, 1909. The cement mill looms large and white at the top left (with the dam
under construction out of sight further to the left), and O'Rourke's Camp is on the hillside in the
middle background. (Courtesy of the Salt River Project)

After the rains abated, Postmaster Burtis received permission to move the post office to Government Hill. The stage company relocated to Newtown and was joined by new shops and services including a telephone company office, an optometrist, a photographer, a dairy, a bakery, an ice cream and soda shop, and at least one new restaurant (figs. 2.13, 2.14, and 2.15).

In 1910, after the peak of construction activity, federal census takers counted only 645 people living in the Roosevelt area. Once the dam was completed and dedicated in 1911, the construction workers left Newtown, Government Hill, and O'Rourke's Camp, and the area's population dropped to only about 250, perhaps a tenth of the peak population. Maintenance and operation employees continued to live on Government Hill, but the Reclamation Service headquarters building is the only construction-era building still standing.

None of Newtown's buildings remain, although there is still a small community on the site catering to the needs of fishermen and boaters on Roosevelt Lake. The owners of the Roosevelt Mercantile Company in Newtown, M. C. Webb and his son A. Cone Webb, bought most of O'Rourke's Camp and turned it into a tourist resort that became known as Hotel Point. A two-story wood-frame building was converted into the Roosevelt Lodge, later called the Apache Hotel, symbolizing the close of the construction era and the opening of the tourist era at Roosevelt.

Camps Dyer and Pleasant

The Roosevelt construction communities fascinated Arizona residents in the first decade of the 1900s, but they were not the only temporary dam-construction communities to appear on the central Arizona landscape. An earlier camp housed workers at the Dyer Diversion Dam northwest of Phoenix between 1892 and 1895. This camp on the east bank of the Agua Fria River was far different from the later Roosevelt communities. In contrast to the more socially complete Roosevelt communities, Camp Dyer was more typical of those that were home to the frontier wageworkers of the last half of the nineteenth century (Schwantes 1987). Camp Dyer was occupied by single men or men away from their families, living in conditions that can be described as little more than primitive.

Irrigation entrepreneur William Beardsley employed twenty to thirty laborers in early 1892 when work began on the Dyer Diversion Dam. By January 1893, thirty to forty employees of the Agua Fria Construction Company had "pitched a camp" of tents or tent houses (Maricopa County Records 1927b). These laborers cleared the sites for the diversion dam and an upstream water storage dam, opened a quarry, and cut rock. In late 1894, construction began on the rock masonry diversion dam itself.

Less than a year later, in October 1895, a flood damaged the unfinished diversion dam, washed away construction equipment, and toppled the construction effort that had been teetering on the brink of financial insolvency. Workers abandoned Camp Dyer after excavating only four miles of the planned thirty-two-mile Beardsley Canal, and the diversion dam stood unfinished and inoperable (fig. 2.16).

Court records stemming from the laborers' efforts to collect their final wages indicate that more than 125 men were employed when the work stopped, and almost all of them were having part of their wages deducted for "board" or a "board and store account" (Maricopa County Records 1896a, 1896b). The small settlement of Frog Tanks (or Pratt) was about a mile upriver, but it was little more than a stage stop. The closest town, Marinette, was at least a half day's ride by wagon or horseback, and it would have taken a couple more hours to get to Phoenix (*Phoenix Daily Herald* [*PDH*] 17 Dec 1891). The deductions for food and the remoteness of the site strongly suggest that all of the workers at the Dyer Diversion Dam lived in Camp Dyer. The archaeological record of the camp supports the conclusion that there were no women or children at the camp during the 1890s.

Some of the laborers lived in tents, and others in a simple frame bunkhouse. Even the wooden building would have offered little insulation from the summer heat and winter chill, and if typical of the times, it was probably infested with lice and fleas. Piles of trash at the site indicate that much of the workers' daily diet came from tin cans, and we can surmise that the food was neither elegant nor diverse. There is no evidence of a well or water system (the men probably used water directly from the river), nor any indication that even pit latrines were used. There was no electrical service. Residential areas were mingled with work areas, so even the powderhouse where explosives were stored was very near some of the living areas. Archaeological recovery of scores of alcoholic beverage bottles suggests that one of the tents sheltered a saloon, perhaps run by an entrepreneurial camp follower who may have monopolized the camp's leisure activities.

FIGURE 2.13 After the old town of Roosevelt was destroyed by floods in late 1908, merchants and residents erected Newtown above the waters of the new lake. This photograph features the Roosevelt Mercantile Company, the only two-story building in the new town. (Courtesy of the National Archives)

FIGURE 2.14 This 1909 photograph of the main street in the new town of Roosevelt includes a side view of the two-story Roosevelt Mercantile Company building, which also housed the Roosevelt Hotel. (Photograph by Walter Lubken, courtesy of the National Archives)

FIGURE 2.15 The Roosevelt Boarding House and the English Kitchen, circa 1909, overlook the rising waters of the new Lake Roosevelt. Both businesses were forced to relocate when the original town of Roosevelt was flooded in late 1908. (Courtesy of the Salt River Project)

A few laborers returned to Camp Dyer some three decades later when Lake Pleasant Dam was constructed between 1926 and 1927 and the Dyer Diversion Dam finally was completed. Most of the 1920s workers lived at Camp Pleasant, about a mile north, at the base of the dam. The camp and the lake were named for the project manager, Carl Pleasant, not for the ambience. As many as six hundred men were employed at the peak of construction, and many of them brought their families. The camp had a population of perhaps a thousand, and its own post office and school.

Camp Pleasant was planned in considerable detail, echoing the precision of the Reclamation Service structures on Government Hill at Roosevelt. Frame buildings and tent houses marched up the hillsides in defiance of the local topography. The camp was divided into functionally discrete zones—that is, the work area, public area, and residential areas were close but separated. There was no powderhouse in the middle of the residential area as there had been at the primitive Camp Dyer some three decades earlier. The camp's public area had a large mess hall, a store, a recreation hall, two large bunkhouses for single men, two bathhouses, a hospital, and the school (fig. 2.17). A group of nineteen frame houses provided living quarters for senior personnel (fig. 2.18), but the project man-ager, Carl Pleasant, lived in a posh Phoenix neighborhood and commuted daily to the camp. Single men lived in tent houses. Almost seventy-five of these tent houses were erected in four different clusters, each laid out with military precision (fig. 2.19). Another twenty tent houses, somewhat larger and more widely spaced, were set up in a separate area for workers living with their families.

Camp Pleasant had a clean-water system, and sewer systems with septic tanks served the bathhouses and the frame houses, which were equipped with indoor plumbing. The residents of the tent houses had access to water hydrants throughout the camp, but they had to walk to the bathhouses or use a pit latrine in the family tent house area. Camp Pleasant also had electrical service, and even the tent houses had at least one electric light, although the frequent recovery of kerosene lamp chimneys suggests the service may have been unreliable. The core of the camp must have been kept relatively clean because huge trash dumps were found on the camp's margins. Nevertheless, there was still a substantial number of lost and discarded items for archaeologists to collect.

Archaeological evidence, historical photographs, and oral testimony indicate that Camp Pleasant's population must have

FIGURE 2.16 William Beardsley posed on top of the Dyer Diversion Dam in 1903 to promote his water storage dam and irrigation project on the Agua Fria River. The buildings of Camp Dyer and the wooden Lidgerwood cableway tower are visible in the background. (Schuyler 1903)

RAISING ARIZONA'S DAMS

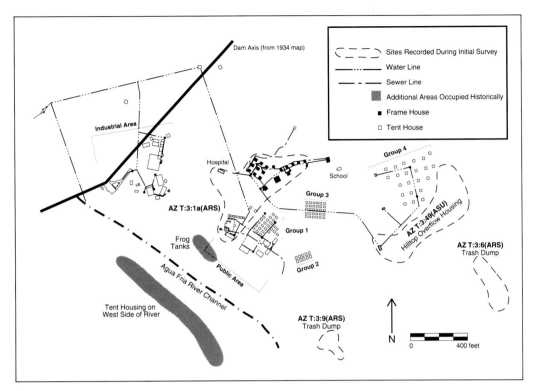

FIGURE 2.17 This map of Camp Pleasant combines four "layers" of information. The base is from a 1926 plan of Camp Pleasant showing housing and work areas laid out with military precision. A second layer of data was provided by a 1934 map prepared when Camp Pleasant was reoccupied to make safety modifications to the dam. This map depicted the dam axis, which allowed the spatially untethered 1926 map to be tied to a known benchmark. The third layer of information depicts archaeological sites designated prior to our field investigations. Because of terrain disturbance, parts of the camp could not be detected archaeologically, and the archaeological evidence of the tent housing areas was so subtle that they also had not been recognized. On the other hand, the archaeological record revealed trash dumps and overflow housing that had not been historically documented. The fourth layer includes the original stage stop at Frog Tanks and another overflow housing area for Camp Pleasant on the west side of the Agua Fria River. These areas are minimally documented by records and photographs but have not been recorded archaeologically. (Courtesy of Dames & Moore)

exceeded the planners' estimates because overflow housing was developed on a ridge south of the main camp and also on the west side of the river. Overflow housing was developed haphazardly in contrast to the planned portions of the camp, and residents undoubtedly did not have some of the camp amenities such as piped-in water and electrical service.

Other Dams, Other Camps

The historical and archaeological record is sketchy for the temporary construction camps at the other three dams built on the Salt River in the 1920s and at the two dams built on the Verde River in the 1930s and 1940s.

The first of these dams, Mormon Flat, was constructed between 1923 and 1926 by laborers hired directly by the Salt River Valley Water Users' Association. Approximately 175 men initiated the work, but eventually about 225 laborers worked at the dam. No map of the camp survives, perhaps because one was never made, but the camp reportedly included three bunkhouses, a mess hall, houses for engineers and superintendents, a reading room, a recreation hall, an ice plant, a bathhouse and ambulance garage, and other sheds for a blacksmith shop, carpenter shop, and cement storage (Introcaso 1989). There is little evidence that workers brought their families to Mormon Flat.

Many of the workers who helped build Mormon Flat probably transferred to the Horse Mesa Dam, which was built by the Water Users' Association between 1924 and 1927. However, the work force for this dam grew to approximately 700 men. The dam site's extremely rugged terrain and sheer canyon walls offered few choices for locating the camp. The first engineers to survey the area lived in caves along the banks of the Salt River (fig. 2.20). Eventually, however, facilities were scattered for a mile downstream of the new dam, on both sides of the river. Approximately twenty buildings were erected, including an ice plant, machine shop, blacksmith shop, carpenter shop, bunkhouses, and a schoolhouse, indicating that the workers' families were part of this construction community (Introcaso 1989). Archaeological evidence indicates that some of the laborers used tent houses, and that some of these were occupied by Apache laborers.

In 1928, a year after the completion of Horse Mesa Dam, construction of Stewart Mountain Dam began, and it is likely that the Salt River Valley Water Users' Association employed at least some of the same laborers. The work force at Stewart Mountain, the lowest and last irrigation storage dam built on the Salt River, peaked at about three hundred. The camp included a mess hall, a timekeeper's office, storeroom, shop, first-aid station, bathhouse, commissary, and an ice house. Single men lived in forty-three six-man bunkhouses designed to minimize disruption for crews working different shifts, and to limit

FIGURE 2.18 This is probably the house occupied by J. G. Tripp, the senior resident construction supervisor at Camp Pleasant, circa 1926. The surprisingly well furnished living room includes typically Arizonan decorating touches: Navajo rugs on the floor and a Pima basket on the table. An issue of *Engineering News* protrudes from a magazine rack. (Courtesy of Herb and Dorothy McLaughlin Historical Collection)

the spread of contagious diseases by dividing the work force into small groups. Some fifty to sixty tent houses were put up for families, and a contemporary source described these family dwellings as segregated into white, Mexican, and Indian areas (Jackson and Fraser 1992b). Maricopa County established a school at the camp for forty pupils (*Arizona Producer* [AP] 1 Apr 1930).

During the 1930s, construction crews returned to each of the 1920s dams on the Salt River to modify them and increase their spillway capacities. The arch buttresses were strengthened and the spillway was modified at Lake Pleasant Dam in the mid-1930s as well. Little is known about these reoccupations of the temporary camps, but all seem to have involved smaller work forces and shorter construction periods than the original occupations.

For the 1937–1938 work at Mormon Flat, the Salt River Valley Water Users' Association and the Bureau of Reclamation cooperated in building four permanent homes for Reclamation engineers. The construction contractor built a camp for only thirty-five men. The rest of the labor force commuted from the almost abandoned mining town of Goldfield, approximately ten miles from the dam site, and others stayed in "tourist camps" on the forest reserve. However, because this was during the Great Depression, there was probably nothing touristy about these camps. They were much more likely make-do homes of families living in desperate circumstances reminiscent of the Joad family described in John Steinbeck's novel *The Grapes of Wrath*.

Approximately 250 men returned to Horse Mesa Dam from September 1936 through November 1937. Little else is known about this reoccupation, but some of the original facilities were

FIGURE 2.19 In this 1927 photo of Camp Pleasant, looking north to the nearly completed dam, tent houses are visible in the left foreground, and frame houses (with canvas window coverings) are on the right. (Courtesy of Herb and Dorothy McLaughlin Historical Collection)

still intact and probably reused; many were not demolished until new housing was built in the 1940s for about ten families that stayed on as the operation and maintenance staff. One bunkhouse stood until the late 1980s.

Crews returned to Stewart Mountain in 1935–1936, but almost no historical or archaeological evidence of the reoccupied camp survives. Once the original dam construction was completed, the original construction camp, located on national forest lands, was leased and converted into a dude ranch. When the ranch was developed for tourists, many of the buildings were moved and modified and probably were not available for reuse by the construction crews of the 1930s. The dude ranch, which continues to operate as the Saguaro Lake Guest Ranch, has achieved its own historic significance and has been proposed for listing on the National Register of Historic Places.

The best documented of the 1930s temporary dam construction communities in central Arizona is the camp at Bartlett Dam, built between 1936 and 1939. Few historical photographs survive, especially in comparison to the photographic record of Camp Pleasant and the Roosevelt camps, but a 1937 map indicates that the camp at Bartlett was carefully planned (fig. 2.21). It was divided into separate sections, one for the construction contractor's employees, and one for the engineers and inspectors employed by the Bureau of Reclamation, which was responsible for designing and constructing the dam before turning it over to the Salt River Valley Water Users' Association for operation and maintenance (see "Floods and Rattlesnakes," p. 72).

By the end of August 1936, the contractor's section of the camp was outfitted with several wood-frame public buildings, including a mess hall, a commissary, a recreation room (complete with billiard parlor), a hospital, a schoolhouse, and a service station. Housing consisted of three wood-frame dormitories, each designed for sixty men, and fifteen three-room, wood-frame houses for families. The contiguous Bureau of Reclamation camp had a six-room house, five four-room

FIGURE 2.20 Before bunkhouses were built at Horse Mesa, survey engineers lived temporarily in caves along the bank of the Salt River. (Courtesy of the Arizona State Archives, *Dam Projects: Box 1, File 13: Arizona State Archives, Department of Library, Archives and Public Records*)

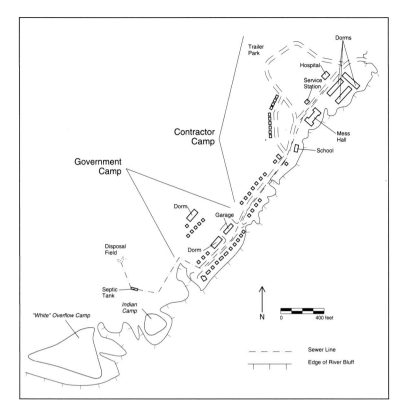

FIGURE 2.21 Plans for the camp at Bartlett Dam included separate sections for the employees of the Bureau of Reclamation and those of the private construction company that won the contract to build the dam. However, as at Camp Pleasant, a larger-than-anticipated work force overflowed into additional housing areas. This 1937 map shows a tent camp area for the contractor's employees that was added at the southwest end of the site, and a separate section that housed Indian workers. A new type of housing, a mobile home trailer park, was also established to house some of the workers. Oral history accounts suggest that workers resided in other undocumented areas that may have been inundated later by the reservoir. (Adapted from Bureau of Reclamation drawings, courtesy of Dames & Moore)

houses, four two-room houses, a twenty-man dormitory, and a garage/warehouse/shop building. Two tent-house churches and a ballpark were also a part of the community (Clapp 1938).

The work force peaked at approximately seven hundred laborers, evidently much higher than anticipated because accommodations had to be made for additional residents. The bureau and the construction contractor added three more dormitories, at least a dozen more houses, and a new form of housing, a trailer park, where about twenty-five families set up mobile homes. (Trailer homes also were a part of the 1934–1935 reoccupation at Camp Pleasant [Bilyeu 1987; Starr 1987].)

Despite these additions, even more overflow housing had to be developed beyond the formal camp. The overflow area was divided into "white" and "Indian" areas (Introcaso 1990; U.S. Bureau of Reclamation 1930–1945). Archaeological evidence in the white area revealed the locations of about a dozen and a half tent houses, a communal latrine, and a shower facility. Historic documentation suggests that more than two dozen families lived in this area, and oral history indicates some families lived in other areas not documented archaeologically or historically (see "The Prices at Bartlett," p. 76).

Archaeological evidence of eleven possible tent house locations was discovered in the Indian area of the camp, corresponding well with limited historical documentation that suggests a dozen families lived there. The archaeological record of this section of the camp was meager, providing few clues about the ethnicity of the residents, but these Indians were very likely Yavapais from the Fort McDowell Reservation, about ten miles downstream. Although Indians were part of the construction community at Bartlett, they constituted no more than a few percent of the work force, a far different situation than at Roosevelt some three decades earlier.

The camp at Horseshoe Dam, occupied between 1944 and 1946 when the dam was constructed, and reoccupied sometime between 1949 and 1951 when spillway gates were added, is the most recent of the dam construction camps of central Arizona. Surprisingly, less is known about this camp than the earlier ones. The wartime effort at Horseshoe Dam did not catch the journalistic fancy of Phoenicians as did the earlier dams. This camp, like Bartlett, was thoroughly cleaned after the dam was finished, leaving few archaeological traces.

There is no good documentation of the nature of the work force, but one historian has speculated that "given the wartime labor shortage that prompted the selection of an earth core and rockfill design, it is doubtful that the work force exceeded one hundred men at any one time, and even this may be a generous estimate" (Jackson and Fraser 1991:42). The rockfill design would not have required the labor-intensive concrete forms needed for the other post-Roosevelt dams, and much of the work had become mechanized by the 1940s (fig. 2.22).

The few surviving photographs of the camp depict at least one large flat-roofed dormitory, and archaeological evidence suggests that about fifteen buildings were erected on concrete slab foundations. Facilities probably included a mess hall, offices, and shops, as well as residential buildings. One photograph depicts a small building labeled as a hospital with a uniformed nurse standing in front of an ambulance. Photographs also depict almost twenty closely spaced tents in three straight rows (fig. 2.23). Only one of these is the older-style tent house. The others are pyramidal tents typical of those used by soldiers during World War II. What appears to be a row of mobile trailers also is visible on the edge of the camp.

Archaeological Insights

The archaeological record of the historic dam construction camps of central Arizona fits the pattern that historian Daniel Boorstein insightfully perceived a quarter century ago. Boorstein characterized the historic archaeology of America as a record of "fast-moving men . . . spread plain and thin on the surface" (Ascher 1974:12). The scatters of artifacts left behind are typically thought of as trash, and they usually are, although some have been unintentionally lost. However, being labeled trash does not mean the artifacts lack potential to yield valuable archaeological information (see "Reading Tin Cans," p. 80, and "Bottles and Bottlenecks," p. 82).

The earthen platforms where tent houses once stood were the most common feature recorded at the construction camps. They offer little potential for what is commonly considered buried archaeological treasures, and they certainly present a challenge in turning "thin" archaeology into "thick" history (Worster 1992:32–33). The archaeology of tent house platforms is a new area of historical archaeological research, and appropriate methodologies are still being developed.

When the camp was first discovered, the tent house locations at Camp Pleasant had not been recognized as archaeological features. Subsequent historical research unearthed a 1926 plan of Camp Pleasant in the files of the Maricopa Water District, and this map provided crucial clues about where to search for the extremely subtle archaeological remnants of tent houses. Once the field crews learned what to look for, tent house features were identified at most of the other construction camps as well. This learning experience also proved to be useful in eventually recognizing the archaeological evidence of Apache wickiups.

The physical evidence of tent houses varies considerably from one earthen platform to another, depending on the size, extent of framing, and the nature of the foundations, which ranged from simple cleared areas, occasionally delineated by rock alignments, to leveled platforms cut into a hillside, often

. . . curios and relics have long been the stuff of "pots-and-pans history," playthings for antiquaries. Now by scrutinizing the mundane events of everyday life for patterns of behavior that reveal a people's basic living conditions and cultural values, social historians have invested ordinary artifacts with new meaning.
—Barbara G. Carson
and Cary Carson
(1983:190)

FIGURE 2.22 The use of air hammers and bulldozers reflects the mechanization of dam construction by the 1940s. (Courtesy of the Salt River Project)

FIGURE 2.23 The bunkhouses and tents in this November 1944 photo of the Horseshoe Dam construction camp were built quickly, and dismantled just as fast after completion of the project. In many ways, the camp had an appearance similar to contemporaneous World War II military camps. (Courtesy of the Salt River Project)

supported on the downslope edge by retaining walls. These walls varied from jumbled rows of rocks to neatly trimmed dry-laid masonry. Pieces of guy wires or tent stakes were some of the best confirming evidence, but they were rarely found (fig. 2.24).

The archaeological record of these tent house features proved to be largely limited to the surface of the ground, but searching on hands and knees near tent house platforms often revealed higher-than-expected artifact densities. For example, more than 10,000 items representing an estimated minimum 9,338 artifacts were recovered from a group of tent houses identified as Cluster 3 at Camp Pleasant. This represents an average of one artifact for about every two square feet of ground surface, or more than 300 artifacts for each of the thirty tent houses that once stood in the area. However, 84 percent of the recovered artifacts are nails, and almost all of the others are quite small.

Although the recovered nails convey some information about the structures that once stood on the earthen platforms, they are unexpectedly not good indicators for distinguishing between simple frame buildings and tent houses. At Camp Pleasant, for example, almost twice as many nails were recovered at platforms where tent houses once stood than at platforms of more substantial frame houses. The large number of nails probably reflects how the camp was abandoned. The tent frames appear to have been dismantled quickly, and the nails probably were pulled and left when the lumber was salvaged. In contrast, some oral history indicates that many of the frame houses were moved to be reused elsewhere.

Other than nails, an average of forty artifacts were found at each of the Cluster 3 tent houses. Fully a third of these (thirteen per tent house) were personal items, dominated by pieces of clothing such as shoe parts (particularly eyelets and heel washers and nails), buttons, belt buckles, rivets, suspender parts, and other clothing fasteners. Also recovered were grooming items such as razor blades, shaving cream tubes, shaving mugs, talcum powder containers, combs, hair tonic bottles, hand mirrors, and nail files. Other personal items include pocket watches and pieces of jewelry such as cuff links.

An average of seven artifacts per tent house represent tools and hardware, including files, hacksaw blades, folding wooden rules, wrenches, drill bits, screws, springs, hose fittings, wire, links of chain, cotter pins, corrugated fasteners, box straps, hardware cloth, grommets, and plumbing pipe. Typically, six artifacts per tent house reflect various leisure and recreation activities, and include tobacco and snuff containers, metal tags from plug tobacco, liquor and soda bottles, malt extract cans, cartridges, harmonica parts, and phonograph records. An average of four artifacts are medical and health items such as aspirin boxes, ointment or salve tubes, toothpaste tubes, eyeglass lenses, adhesive tape spools, and various prescription and proprietary medicine bottles.

About three items per platform are architectural artifacts other than nails, including window screen and window screen springs, window glass, hinges, electrical wire, and insulators. An average of three artifacts are food containers, mostly general food cans, although the original contents of a few cans and bottles could be more specifically identified. Household furnishings and transportation are reflected by an average of a single artifact per tent house. These include artifacts such as cot parts, stove parts, electrical bulbs, kerosene lamp chimneys, and mirrors. Most of the transportation artifacts are related to automobiles, including tire patches, valve stems, engine parts, and lightbulbs. A few horseshoe nails and harness snaps reflect the continuing use of horses.

Collections from the nearby group of twenty-two more widely spaced tent house platforms, labeled Cluster 4, yielded almost 14,000 artifacts, or an average of more than 600 hundred per tent house—twice as many as at Cluster 3. Although the average number of nails was similar (260 versus 298), the larger average number of artifacts per tent house suggests more intense use of the area, an interpretation consistent with the identification of this area as one where families resided.

The wives and children of workers would have spent a considerable amount of time in the tent house area while laborers were at work. The functional profile of the collection in the family area also was quite different. More than half of the average of 266 non-nail artifacts per tent house are food containers or food preparation and consumption artifacts, supporting the identification of this area as the residences of families who prepared their own meals, in contrast to the single men who ate most of their meals in the mess hall (see "The Archaeology of Food," p. 84).

Other artifacts such as baby bottles and toys are more specific indicators of the presence of children (fig. 2.25). For example, an average of five such artifacts were recovered from each tent at the family tent house cluster at Camp Pleasant, and none were found at Cluster 3.

Some artifacts reflect the presence of women, but a few are

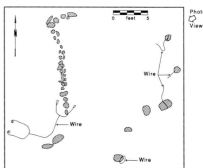

FIGURE 2.24 A field photograph and sketch map of feature 20 depict the scant archaeological evidence indicating an "obvious" tent platform and attest to the difficulties of some types of historical archaeological fieldwork. (Courtesy of Dames & Moore)

ambiguous. Garter clasps might reflect use by men to hold up socks instead of by women to hold up undergarments, and although women's shoes were more commonly fastened with buttons, some button hooks might have been used by men, particularly for dress shoes. Artifacts that more definitely suggest the presence of women at the Roosevelt camps include corset stays, corset lacing strips, hand mirrors, and cosmetic bottles. At Camp Pleasant, garter clasps replace corset stays, and a lipstick tube, beads, hairpins, and purse frames also indicate the presence of women (fig. 2.26). Fortunately, historical documentation can be used to augment archaeological evidence of women and children in the dam construction camps.

Women and Children in the Camps

Women have been neglected as a topic by the same romantic and mythical notions that have affected all of Western history. As Sandra Myres points out, quoting T. A. Larson, women "did not lead expeditions, command troops, build railroads, drive cattle, ride Pony Express, find gold, amass great wealth, get elected to high public office, rob stages or lead lynch mobs" (1983:369). Nor, it might be added, did they engage in wage labor on dam construction projects, but clearly women did

Clearly the outstanding contribution of American women from every religious and racial group has been as community builders.
—ELIZABETH H. PLECK
(1983:52)

other important types of work in many of the dam construction camps of central Arizona.

There is virtually no archaeological evidence of women and children at the 1892–1895 Camp Dyer, and this is consistent with the classification of this camp as representative of the last of the frontier wageworker camps, which were typically occupied only by men. The population of the West was by no means so dominated by men (Bartlett 1974), because adult males constituted 40 percent of the Arizona Territory population in 1890 and 1900. In contrast, women made up 20 percent of the population. According to the 1910 census, almost three of every four residents of O'Rourke's Camp at Roosevelt were male—a lingering indication of the wage-laborer frontier. However, about half of the counted Roosevelt construction community were adult men, about 20 percent adult women, and almost 30 percent children, which was fairly representative of the territorial population. Women certainly were an important component of the total Roosevelt Dam construction community.

The historical record of the Roosevelt Dam construction community provides the best information regarding the activities of women in the dam construction camps of central Arizona. Newspaper stories mention a schoolteacher, an amateur dentist, several boarding-house operators, the *de facto* postmistress, and a traveling merchant. The 1910 census taker also recorded other working women, including a cook for a family, a hotel chambermaid, servants, laundresses, gardeners, and stenographers. Other roles for women at Roosevelt might be presumed, such as midwife.

Operating boarding houses to feed Roosevelt workers seems to have been a common endeavor for entrepreneurial women. Several women established boarding houses (offering both room and board) and restaurants, presumably for single men (AR 5 Nov 1907, 4 Feb 1909, 16 May 1909). Mrs. D. McCauley started up a restaurant "in the old Parker tent," and her dozen boarders in 1909 looked "contented and homey." Mrs. Will McCauley, possibly a sister-in-law, assisted as a specialist in pastry, and Mrs. Braddock of Livingston supplied fresh hens to this restaurant "down near the dam" (AR 9 May 1909, 6 June 1909).

Another, larger boarding operation was described by Sallie Pemberton in her memoirs. She and her husband, George, had come to Arizona from Missouri in 1886. When construction began on the Roosevelt power canal, the contractor requested

FIGURE 2.25 Artifacts indicating the presence of children at some of the dam construction camps include toys, doll dishes, marbles, a toy car, and a child's alphabet mug. (Courtesy of Dames & Moore)

that Sallie set up a boarding facility nearby for twenty-five men. She agreed, establishing a large mess hall with tables and a big stove. Pemberton eventually served as many as sixty men, for whom she daily cooked hot meals; baked bread, pies, and cakes; and prepared lunches. Twice a month, she drove a wagon on the two-day trip to Globe to buy flour, bacon, and notions. Fresh meat, fruit, and vegetables were delivered by neighbors. Pemberton and her husband later moved downstream to the Roosevelt area and lived in a tent house below the cement mill, where he worked as a subforeman (Salt River Project Archives 1956).

Some women worked as domestics for more prosperous residents, although the extent of this practice is not clear. Dr. Palmer's diary reveals that some of the wives of the African American laborers brought by O'Rourke from Texas worked as servants on Government Hill. One of them was "a very good cook and nurse as she took care of Harriet, our second child,

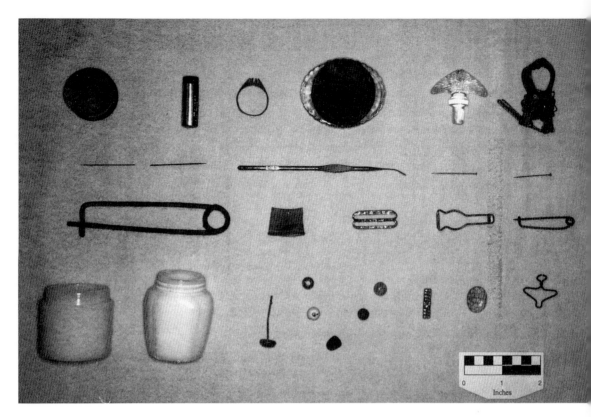

FIGURE 2.26 A rouge container, lipstick holder, a ring, beads and other items of jewelry, a stopper from a lost perfume bottle, a crochet hook, knitting stitch holders, pins and needles, a smashed thimble, garter clasps, and milk glass jars that once contained cold cream are artifacts that indicate the presence of women at some of the construction camps. (Courtesy of Dames & Moore)

when she came along in October 1905" (Palmer 1979:125).

The 1910 census reveals that most women were married, and few women worked outside their homes. All of the twenty-four adult women at O'Rourke's Camp were wives of engineers, foremen, blacksmiths, or common laborers. All but two of the adult women living on Government Hill were married to engineers, foremen, laborers, and tradesmen (machinists, electricians, carpenters, miners in the rock quarry, postmaster, surveyors). Only two women in O'Rourke's Camp, both African American, were identified as having occupations. One was listed as a laundress and the other as a washerwoman; each was married to an African American laborer. A third African American wife took four lodgers into her home. Only two women living on Government Hill were unmarried; one worked as a cook for a family, and the other as a stenographer. One of the married women living on Government Hill also worked as a stenographer.

More women lived in Newtown than in any of the other camps counted in the census. Reflecting the town's entreprencurial tone, seven of the fifty-six Newtown women were identified as having occupations. One was a merchant, another was a chambermaid, two were servants, and three were laundresses. Two of the three laundresses were born in Mexico; the third was an Anglo woman, head of a household with four children. None of the eleven Indian women counted at Newtown were listed as being employed.

There is little indication that women were employed at the other camps, but this may be due to the limits of the historic documentation. An occasional picture depicts a woman working in a mess hall (Horse Mesa Dam) or as a nurse (Horseshoe Dam), or school records identify them as teachers (Camp Pleasant). One 1930s laborer remembered that the women in camp cooked, fixed lunches, and "just made our life a little easier." He also suggested that families located themselves apart from the single men at Camp Pleasant to avoid exposure to the "cussing and whatnot" (Horton 1986).

Roosevelt Damsite Doings

Social life in the Roosevelt communities was reported in the Phoenix and Globe newspapers on a regular basis. Headlines such as "Damsite Doings," "News from the Basin," or "Storage Basin News" introduced human interest stories about baseball games, dances, church services, and just plain gossip. A local newspaper called the *Roosevelt Tattler* was published for a time, but unfortunately, no surviving copies have been located (Zarbin 1984).

Roosevelt was not isolated from the outside world. A post office was established early in the project, and daily mail service was in operation between Globe and Roosevelt by August 1904, and between Mesa and Roosevelt by December of that year. The established businesses of Roosevelt were augmented by traveling merchants who periodically brought their wares to the Tonto Basin. Mr. Wasserman came from Globe in 1908 to see the dam and to sell ribbons and laces "to the ladies" (AR 28 June 1908). Mr. Anderson, an "old timer" who had owned a ranch on "the Eddy Flat" covered by the new lake, became a merchant selling candies and cakes (AR 6 June 1909). Establishments in Newtown and at O'Rourke's sold ice

[Roosevelt] is taking on quite a metropolitan air.
—EARL A. ZARBIN
(1984:96, quoting the *Arizona Republican*, January 21, 1905)

cream and soda water (*Arizona Gazette* [AG] 16 June 1908; AR 21 June 1908). The town of Roosevelt had several restaurants, a bakery, pool hall, laundry, ice-cream parlor, hot springs, and for a time at least, a bowling alley. Opened by 1905, the Monarch Bowling Alley closed in August 1906 when proprietor Bert Royce could not afford to pay the monthly Gila County license fee of $30 due to slow summer business (AR 12 Nov 1905). A newspaper reporter lamented the loss of the alley because "the Royce place was popular among the young men and afforded them a place to spend their evenings pleasantly" (AR 12 Aug 1906).

Although alcoholic beverages were prohibited at Reclamation Service project sites, they were regularly smuggled in and brewed or distilled locally (AR 13 Oct 1905, 6 June 1909). To drink legally, workers had to find saloons outside the limits of the Reclamation Service project, such as those at Tortilla Flat and Mormon Flat on the Apache Trail (AR 29 June 1905).

Baseball games were another form of recreation, and generally, teams were organized along ethnic and racial lines (AR 11 Oct 1908). Anglo Reclamation Service engineers, office personnel, and laborers fielded a team, as did the Apaches and the Mexicans (AR 3 Apr 1904). A newspaper reported at least one exception to the rigid racial and ethnic makeup of baseball teams. One week in 1908, Anglo Bert Henderson acted as umpire in a baseball game between the Apaches and the Mexicans, and a week later, he pitched for the Apache team (AR 11 Oct 1908, 18 Oct 1908). The Reclamation Service team also played against teams in Globe and Mesa (AR 13 Mar 1905, 20 Apr 1905).

Other Roosevelt sports included tennis and basketball. Government Hill had a grass tennis court where singles and mixed doubles tournaments were held for both men and women (AR 21 Mar 1906). Women's basketball teams were organized at O'Rourke's Camp; one newspaper made note of the ladies playing their "usual" game one evening, with the Whitecaps defeating the Redcaps 6-2 (AG 16 June 1908).

Other outdoor recreation included hunting for wildcats, mountain lions, rabbits, quail, and doves (AR 27 Nov 1905, 18 Oct 1908, 27 June 1909, 17 Nov 1909). After the new reservoir began filling in 1908, residents enjoyed sport fishing (AR 30 May 1909; *Arizona Silver Belt* [ASB] 14 Apr 1909).

A "huge crowd" of Roosevelt residents attended an April 1904 horse race (AR 14 Apr 1904). On another occasion, horse racing was combined with two other Roosevelt recreations, baseball and gambling; "quite a bit of money" was said to have been lost on a two-horse race scheduled just before a baseball game (AR 11 Oct 1909, 18 Oct 1908). Card games such as poker sometimes involved gambling, although the law forbade playing cards for drinks or "any other consideration" (AR 12 Aug 1906; Shute 1909).

Other card games were more genteel. In 1906, "some gentlemen of Roosevelt-on-the Hill" hosted a "progressive whist party in honor of their lady friends." They decorated the "assembly hall" with mistletoe and "greens," served a fruit punch during the card playing, and offered a buffet lunch at the conclusion of the games (AR 14 Jan 1906).

Roosevelt residents swam in several locales, including Tonto Creek, the Salt River, a hot springs near the base of the new dam, and the new reservoir. In 1905 and 1906, E. E. Bacon operated the hot springs for laundry and bathing customers, but the operation was flooded out in 1906 (Zarbin 1984). As the reservoir began to fill, new tourists began to share Roosevelt Lake with the local residents. In response to this new market, local merchants expanded their lines of bathing suits, although some of the boys were known to be swimming naked in the dim light at dusk (AR 30 May 1909, 6 June 1909).

Roosevelt residents held dances all over the Tonto Basin, at old Roosevelt, Government Hill, O'Rourke's Camp, Newtown, and some of the nearby ranches. The first dances were held at the "town hall" in Roosevelt in early 1904. Soon, local restaurateur Dick Baker constructed a new dance pavilion, known as Baker's Hall, where Saturday-night dances were regularly held. One reporter wrote that a June dance "was attended by a large and fashionable gathering of ladies and gentlemen from all over the valley" (AR 26 June 1904). Weekly dances were also held in the dining hall on Government Hill, usually on Thursdays (AR 31 May 1905, 11 Apr 1909).

O'Rourke's Camp also hosted dances on a regular basis, attracting attendees from the south side of the Salt River. At first, residents of Roosevelt, Newtown, and Government Hill used the footbridge to cross the river. Later, as the reservoir filled, they used boats (AR 28 June 1908, 23 Aug 1909). The Elks Club of Roosevelt held their first annual ball at the recreation hall in O'Rourke's Camp in 1909, sending invitations to their brother lodges throughout the eastern United States, to the Arizona legislature, and even to Theodore Roosevelt (AR 14 Feb 1909). Other diversions at O'Rourke's Camp included a Halloween "Tacky Ball" in 1908, a Thanksgiving Masquerade

Ball a month later, and a "big dance" at the recreation hall as part of the wedding celebration of Miss Elect Carrick and Harry Pierson in June 1908 (AR 9 Nov 1908, 15 Nov 1908, 28 June 1908).

National and ethnic holidays were also occasions for festivities and dancing. On Washington's Birthday in February 1906, the "young people" on Government Hill gave a party with games and dancing in the "assembly hall" (AR 28 Feb 1906). On St. Patrick's Day the next year, "Spud" Murphy went about giving friends pieces of real shamrock from Ireland, and a dance was held in the Newtown hall in the evening (AR 21 Mar 1909). Mexicans celebrated Independence Day on September 16, 1908, with dancing to "excellent music" (AR 20 Sept 1908). Dancing until midnight was also one of the attractions of the Cinco de Mayo celebration the next spring. Although all were welcomed, only a few "Americans" attended, and most departed earlier than expected. The Mexicans were disappointed since they had planned a "feast" with cakes, ice cream, candies, nuts, and other items (AR 9 May 1909).

Several different groups provided music for the many dances, including African American and Mexican musical groups. The "Negro string band" from O'Rourke's Camp played and sang for an appreciative Roosevelt-on-the Hill audience in 1906 and were "well paid" for their effort (AR 12 Aug 1906). The same band played at O'Rourke's in 1908 and at Newtown in 1909 (AR 28 June 1908, 4 Feb 1909). Two Mexicans played at "the usual Thursday night dance" on Government Hill in 1909 (AR 11 Apr 1909).

African Americans and Mexicans were not the only musicians to play at the dances. The Mormon Trio provided mandolin and banjo music for an exclusive affair in January 1906 (AR 20 Jan 1906), and the Roosevelt Peerless Orchestra from O'Rourke's Camp played regularly (AR 5 Mar 1908). Musicians were sometimes brought in from Globe; one trio of men included "a natural born fiddler and proud possessor of a Stradivarius made in 1741," an "accomplished violinist," and a guitarist (AR 23 Aug 1909). In addition to the musicians, a new Victor phonograph and a good selection of records provided concerts for government employees in the east room of the office building (AR 24 Sept 1907).

Over the years, a variety of shows entertained the Roosevelt workers and their families. Touring theater companies visited the area from time to time, performing in Baker's Hall and the

Roosevelt opera house in 1905 and 1906 (AR 27 Nov 1905, 14 Jan 1905, 20 Jan 1906). Local talent also appeared on the stage; a 1908 Christmas Eve play at O'Rourke's Camp, "The Sniggles Family," was written and performed by area residents (AR 3 Jan 1908). "California Joe" brought a traditional Wild West performance to the Tonto Basin in September 1908, complete with fancy rifle shooting, bows and arrows, and live snakes wound around Joe's wife's body (AR 13 Sept 1908, 20 Sept 1908). The next month, "about everyone in camp turned out" to watch the Apache "Devil Dance" at an Indian camp about three miles from Roosevelt. The non-Indian newspaper reporter described six Indian men and a small boy dancing "in a weird way" around a large bonfire while other Indians beat drums and chanted "a funny kind of song" (AR 18 Oct 1908).

The social life of the Roosevelt Dam construction community may have been more varied and elaborate than in many of the smaller, shorter-lived dam construction camps, but life in the camps was never all work and no play. The incorporation of women and children into the camps certainly did much to foster the development of more complete communities.

After the middle of the twentieth century, temporary construction camps became essentially extinct in central Arizona. The speed, ease, and lowered cost of automobile transportation on improved roads now allow construction workers to live in established communities and commute to job sites on a daily basis, in air-conditioned comfort. To be sure, this new approach to construction work offers workers numerous advantages, but it also entails fewer opportunities to build the bonds of teamwork and camaraderie that must have developed in the construction camps.

PHOTOGRAPHS OF DAILY LIFE

Hired by the Reclamation Service to document the construction progress of Roosevelt Dam, Walter Lubken (fig. 2.27) produced hundreds of photographs of the dam as it rose from the canyon floor, but he must have sensed that it was not just the engineering marvels that should be recorded for posterity. Lubken carried his camera throughout the Roosevelt communities, recording details of the daily lives of those who lived in the construction camps (figs. 2.28, 2.29, 2.30, and 2.31).

FLOODS AND RATTLESNAKES

As early as 1889, enterprising residents of the Salt River Valley looked to the Verde River for water. The Rio Verde Canal Company incorporated in 1891 to bring Verde River water to the northern stretches of Maricopa County with a series of dams and canals. Their visionary plans called for irrigating fields from the McDowell Mountains south to Camelback Mountain, and from Cave Creek west to the Hassayampa River. The *San Francisco Chronicle* (23 Apr 1983) reported that the project was "of the greatest magnitude [and] surpass[ed] any similar enterprise in Arizona, and, indeed, in the United States." However, the nationwide financial depression of the 1890s left the company struggling to raise funds for dam and canal construction for the next three decades.

The success of the U.S. Reclamation Service and the Salt River Valley Water Users' Association in constructing the four dams along the Salt River drew attention and support away from the Verde water plan. The more powerful Water Users' Association vigorously opposed the plans of the newly named Verde Irrigation and Power District to establish a separate irrigation district based on Verde River water. With the crash of the national economy in 1929 and then the loss of promised federal monies in 1934, the District collapsed.

The Salt River Valley Water Users' Association wasted no time in laying claim to the dam site eyed for so many years by the District. A month *before* the cancellation of promised federal money forced the collapse of the District, the Water Users' Association had sent two men to guard the Bartlett Dam site until construction could begin. John J. Huber and Orson Boyle

FIGURE 2.27 The gentleman pictured almost certainly is Walter Lubken, who captured himself in the act of photographing the old town of Roosevelt, threatened with flooding as water began to back up behind the rising dam, February 4, 1908. (Courtesy of the National Archives)

FIGURE 2.28 Some students rode a "burro bus" to the Roosevelt school, but most probably walked. (Photograph by Walter Lubken, courtesy of the National Archives)

FIGURE 2.29 Mr. L. Beata
Neves, a Brazilian engi-
neer, inspects Roosevelt
Dam, February 8, 1909,
with Reclamation Service
construction engineer
Chester W. Smith (*left*)
and Howard S. Reed
(*right*), who managed part
of the canal system in the
Salt River Valley for the
Reclamation Service.
(Photograph by Walter
Lubken, courtesy of the
National Archives)

FIGURE 2.31 These men
are killing a rattlesnake
found in Lake Roosevelt,
three hundred yards from
the shore. The new
reservoir drove many
desert creatures from their
homes and altered the
fauna of the river as well.
(Photograph by Walter
Lubken, circa 1910,
courtesy of the National
Archives)

set up a tent on a small island in the Verde River in September 1934, and for the next two years, they represented the Water Users' Association claim on the site.

Whether or not the two men expected to shoot it out with angry shareholders of the Verde Irrigation and Power District is unknown, but the major challenges to their position seem to have been the forces of nature rather than man. In December 1934, only three months after they set up camp, the Verde River rose and threatened to inundate the island. Swift currents prevented Huber and Boyle from reaching the landing on the west bank of the river, so they were forced to climb the steep, rugged cliffs on the east bank. They set up a temporary camp there until the waters finally receded—in mid-February.

Prior to the flood, the two men had walked six miles upriver to get supplies at a gauging station maintained by the Water Users' Association, hauling the goods back to camp on their own backs. During the flood, however, their temporary camp was on the opposite side of the river from the gauging station. Not only did they have to hike the six miles, but to reach the gauging station, they also had to climb a twenty-five-foot pole and cross the river in a bosun's chair attached to a cable. Of course, the return trip across the river included a load of supplies.

When the river receded, the two men made a new camp under a distinctive balancing rock near the dam site. As they cleared the area for their new camp, they also cleared out a couple of dozen rattlers from their winter hibernation quarters.

FIGURE 2.30 (opposite bottom) These young residents of the east side of Newtown were photographed on January 20, 1909, shortly after the town of Roosevelt was relocated. (Photograph by Walter Lubken, courtesy of the National Archives)

Other snakes were less docile. In July 1936, Huber woke up in a lightning storm and heard his dog barking. Turning on his flashlight, he found a rattler on the floor of the tent, coiled and ready to strike. Just as he killed the snake with a stick, a second rattler, larger than the first, slid into the tent. The second reptile met the same fate as the first.

During two years on the site, Huber often caught rattle-snakes with a wire attached to the end of a stick. Once, visiting Bureau of Reclamation survey engineers stewed up a batch of rattlers to see how they would taste.

In addition to fleeing floods and dispatching rattlers, the two Bartlett guards worked to build a road along the path to the gauging station. By spring of 1935, they used two horses to haul supplies, but not always successfully. On one trip, much of the 300 pounds of ice that Huber brought from the gauging station had melted by the time he reached camp. On another trip, he brought a case of eggs to the camp, but on arrival, Huber's excited dog dumped over the entire case. By the time dam construction began in August 1936, giant diesel trucks hauled tons of concrete and steel into the dam site along the same seventeen-mile route.

Boyle was replaced in March 1935 by Paul Greenhaw. Both Greenhaw and Huber stayed on at Bartlett throughout construction of the dam, from "the first diamond drill bite into the rock" until "the last bucket of concrete poured," and they understood "the worry, trouble, hard work, and final construction triumph that the mute mass of sand, stone, cement and steel represents" (AR 12 June 1939).

THE PRICES AT BARTLETT

Historians often use the tools of private investigators to discover information about the past, but sometimes investigations turn on odd bits of good luck. Hoping to find adult children of dam laborers, we compared the 1926–1927 Lake Pleasant school attendance records to the 1986 metropolitan Phoenix telephone book. The January 1928 school register listed eight-year-old Robert Price and six-year-old Russell Price, and in an attempt to locate the Price brothers, we phoned an "R. Price" listed in the telephone book. In his kindly Oklahoma drawl, Mr. Price informed us that he was not related to Robert or Russell, that he did not grow up at Lake Pleasant, and that his father had not been a construction worker on that dam. Before we hung up in

RAISING ARIZONA'S DAMS

disappointment, he went on to say, "But you might be interested in this—I myself worked on the Bartlett Dam." We spoke to Ray and Lee Price in their Phoenix home in October 1986.

Leaving his new wife, Lee, in Oklahoma, twenty-one-year-old Ray Price left the restaurant he owned with his brother and came to Arizona in 1936 looking for construction work. At first, he had trouble getting into the union.

They wouldn't take me in because all the work they had was heavy work, pouring concrete. I had been working inside as a cook so I was white—I didn't have a tan. So I went over to California and worked awhile, and when I came back by, I had a tan and looked like a working man, so they took me into the laborers union.

Price worked for short periods at Stewart Mountain Dam and then at Horse Mesa Dam doing repair work. In 1937, he was hired as a laborer on the construction of Bartlett Dam on the Verde River.

I went to work at the Bartlett Dam for $.50 an hour [about $20.00 a week]. I was paying $10.50 a week for board and room, so that didn't leave me a lot of money. A man with a family, he could stay in Phoenix and work part-time, pick up whatever he could, and do better. So that's why an inexperienced person like myself could find a job at Bartlett.

Lee joined Ray at the dam site in July 1937. Because the planned housing area below the dam was fully occupied, the Prices lived in a tent house in the big wash above the dam (in an area apparently not preserved as an archaeological site). Although the dwelling lacked both electricity and running water, Mrs. Price remembered the newlyweds' desert home with fondness.

We'd been married about six months when we moved to Bartlett. At that time, fifty years ago, there wasn't too many trailers. Wherever you could find a nice tree, you'd set up your tent. Our tent had a floor in it, it had walls, just one room, and my husband had screened it in all the way around. The tent was just really the roof. We had linoleum on the floor. We had a rock fence around it, and we built little paths out to our outside bathroom, and we kept everything just as clean as we would if we lived in a house.

We had little quail that were just like little chickens. They came up all the time for their food. The rabbits would come, too. They would hop all out in our yard. I even had a little pet lizard that stayed up on top of my tent.

We had a little kerosene two-burner stove and a little ice box we had bought here in Phoenix. We had a man up there that delivered ice, he hauled it from Phoenix twice a week. I wasn't used to a real fancy lifestyle. I thought it was just the way of life not to have electricity. I didn't feel like I was cheated because other people didn't have it.

We had to haul our water, both to cook and to wash. We had to haul it from the commissary, which was quite a ways. The wash water—we could get it out of the river. We had a No. 3 galvanized wash tub and we bathed in that. And we bathed as often as we do when you got running water and a shower.

Ray recalled that working in the desert was hard, and he saw "many a man pass out working on the job from the heat." He also remembered one frightening accident in which three workers were fatally crushed by a rock slide.

The Prices didn't remember any women working on the dam or running boardinghouses; only one elderly lady took in laundry for the working men. Lee prided herself on her house-keeping and cooking skills.

Ray was working swing shift, and time we would get up of a morning and have breakfast, he'd do things that he had to do around the place. I'd clean up the house, and then I had to fix dinner for him and then pack his lunch. After he left, I did what chores I had to do. About twice a week, I had to do laundry, and I did laundry for his two brothers. We did our washing on a rub board, in a tub.

I made a lot of my clothes, and I made curtains and things to go around for my windows. I made them all by hand. I have always sewed. Ever since I was a small child, I've sewed.

I baked a whole lot more up there than I do now. I had a little oven that went on top of the stove, and if I do say so, I made delicious cherry pie. We had to do all our baking so he'd have stuff to go in his lunch. When we came into Phoenix, I'd usually always buy enough fresh meat like pork chops or steak to last a couple of days. I'd put 'em right on the ice [in the icebox]. Then I bought a lot of canned lunch meats like Spam, and I bought an awful lot of bacon. That was a lot of his sandwiches, bacon and egg sandwiches. He always had a real nourishing lunch.

Ray bought a used 1931 Model A roadster for $110 shortly after he began working at Bartlett, and the Prices regularly drove into Phoenix to go food shopping.

We came to Phoenix every two weeks and bought our groceries, and in the meantime, if we needed fresh meat and vegetables, we bought it at the commissary store. We bought our milk at the commissary all the time. But it was so much higher and we didn't have a whole lot of money, so we had to come into Phoenix to the Consumers' Wholesale Grocery on Third Street and Jefferson. We came in one day and went back the next.

I never will forget. I went to this store where I always bought groceries at in Phoenix, and there was a young kid in there. I asked the kid for twenty-five pounds of bacon and he just stood there and looked at me. Well, the man that ran the butcher shop, he knew me, and he said, "What's wrong?" And he said, "I thought she said she wanted twenty-five pounds of bacon." And he said, "She did. When she tells you she wants twenty-five pounds of bacon and fifteen dozen eggs, that's what she wants and you get it for her." I had a sister-in-law up there. When she came to town, she'd get for me, and when I'd come to town, then I'd get for her.

Despite the isolation and distance from Phoenix, Lee Price remembered spending pleasant times with friends and neighbors.

We had neighbors around, and we had a lot of friends. Whenever Ray'd have days off, we'd go visit friends that we had up there. We'd gather at first one's house and then another. We'd fix a big dinner and make ice cream.

Not all their outings with friends were happy occasions. Lee described a nerve-wracking return to Bartlett after a social visit to Phoenix.

I'll never forget one time we came into Phoenix with a couple. We had known 'em quite a while, but I had never seen him drunk. We were in their car, and of course that little old road used to be so narrow, and it was all washboardy dirt road, and the more his wife would talk to him about trying to get him to let Ray drive, the faster he got. And I'll tell you, I done a lot of praying from Phoenix to Bartlett. When we got home, Ray said, "Never again. We'll go in our own car from now on."

At the time he left Bartlett, Ray had been promoted to a carpenter's position. In later years, he continued to work in construction, contributing his efforts to Parker Dam on the Colorado River, and the Arizona Biltmore and North High School in Phoenix. In his last big job, Ray did the layout and engineering "from down in the ground to the top" of the new Adams Hotel (now the downtown Holiday Inn). He declared it to be "the plumbest building in town."

Fifty years later, their Bartlett years remained special to the Prices, and Lee smiled as she recalled them.

We had it pretty nice. To me, I think it was the happiest time of our life. We didn't have anything, but we were happy. He had a job—lot of people didn't—and I think that was the most important thing for a young couple starting out being married. I really enjoyed it.

READING TIN CANS

To most people, messy piles of rusty trash dumped in an arroyo or off the edge of a bluff are nothing more than eyesores. Although a historical archaeologist may agree that such piles of trash spoil the beauty of a desert landscape, they also see tin cans and broken dishes and bottles as archaeological records waiting to be read (fig. 2.32).

Upon a careful look inside your kitchen cupboards, it is obvious that soup cans are different than sardine cans, and condensed-milk cans are a different size and shape than a can of Spam. Similarly, a historical archaeologist can use the size and shape of cans to determine the diet of the people who created the dump.

Typically, meat, sardine, and kipper cans have key openings. Cans with puncture holes or church key openings probably contained liquids. Cans with openings that are completely cut around or have "X-cut" lids, with the metal peeled back, were probably fruit and vegetable containers. The size of cans also can indicate whether the dump represents trash from individual households or mess halls or restaurants. Institutions commonly used large No. 10 cans, and when scores of evaporated milk cans are slashed for rapid pouring rather than punctured with a more delicate hole, it suggests an institutional origin.

Some cans are embossed with markings that identify their original contents and brand names, such as baking powder. The "KC" brand of baking powder also was commonly embossed with slogans such as "same price today as 25 years ago" or ". . . 35 years ago." It is known that the price was set in 1890, and so cans with these slogans date to 1915 and 1925, respectively (Ward, Abbink, and Stein 1977). Thus, these cans provide good clues for determining the dates of trash deposits.

However, even unmarked cans provide chronological information because of the evolution of can-manufacturing technology. The idea of "canning" food originated in England in 1810, when Augusta de Heine and Peter Durand patented tin canisters made from tin plate or iron plate that had been cut, shaped, and soldered by hand (Rock 1984). These containers typically were filled through a hole in one end, which was capped and soldered after filling. Because of contamination, these hole-and-cap cans had a tendency to swell and burst.

An initial canning improvement involved puncturing a small vent hole in the cap piece, which could be sealed with a drop of solder after excess air and moisture was driven off (after the can was filled and heated to kill bacteria). These hole-in-cap cans were the first type used for commercial canning in the United States, and daily production rates averaged about sixty cans per tinsmith.

Machines were invented in the 1840s to stamp the end pieces of cans with flanges that could be easily slipped over and more securely soldered to the can cylinders. Large canneries using this improved technology were established in East Coast cities such as Boston and Baltimore. During the Civil War, foods such as sweet corn, chickens, turkeys, ducks, geese, and beef were

FIGURE 2.32 This trash dump, made up mostly of tin cans, was found near the Stewart Mountain Dam construction camp. (Courtesy of Dames & Moore)

packaged in "tin cans," as they had become known in the United States. Salmon canneries had been established on the West Coast by this time. The key-wind opening mechanism was also invented during the 1860s.

The tapered can, used particularly for meat, was developed in the 1870s, but a more significant invention of the decade was the "Howe Floater" system, which automated the soldering of can ends. Soldering of side seams was semiautomated by 1883, and production of as many as 2,500 cans per machine per hour was possible.

In 1888, Max Ams made one of the most significant contributions to the canning industry when he invented a method for interlocking a can's side seam. By 1904, cans were being produced with fully crimped side and end seams, with no solder required for sealing. These so-called sanitary cans are the type still being used today.

The technology of food preservation and canning has continued to advance, and tin cans may not be as popular as they once were, but they have proven to be remarkably durable. Literally millions and millions have been used and discarded over the years, and to a trained eye, those piles of rusty cans are books waiting to be read.

BOTTLES AND BOTTLENECKS

Anyone who has ever walked into an antique store is bound to have noticed shelves lined with old bottles. The diversity of sizes, shapes, and hues has a beauty that attracts collectors—an attraction that unfortunately can lead to the looting of historical archaeological sites. A few of the bottles may have information-laden paper labels, and others may have embossed labeling that identifies the bottle's original contents.

Few whole bottles were recovered from the dam construction camps (fig. 2.33), but some of the broken pieces had sufficient embossing to identify a variety of products. These included patent medicines with such wonderful names as *Scott's Emulsion Cod Liver Oil with Lime & Soda, Dr. Kilmer's Swamp Root Kidney Liver and Bladder Cure, Peruvian Bitters, Hamlin's Wizard Oil, Dr. J. H. McLean's Volcanic Liniment Oil,* and *Gifford and Co. H. H. H. Medicine,* which may have been used to treat the ills of both horses and men. Other embossed marks identify beverages, from forgotten products such as *Waterfill & Frazier Whiskey* to still-common drinks such as *Coca Cola* and

7-Up, and foods such as *Gebhardt Eagle Chili Powder, Lea & Perrins Worcestershire Sauce*, and *Karo Syrup*. Other identifiable products were for personal grooming, such as *Hinds Honey and Almond Cream, Milkweed Cream, Hoyt's German Cologne*, and *Ideal Dandruff Remover*.

Almost five hundred different markings were identified on bottle-glass fragments collected from the dam construction camps, but most of these do not provide obvious identification of the bottle's original contents. Many are rather cryptic initials, but guides (such as Toulouse 1969, 1971) can help identify the manufacturers of the products or the companies who made the bottles themselves. Researchers have determined when many of these marks were in use, and this information can be analyzed to date the occupations of archaeological sites.

Even seemingly plain bottles can provide information. For example, dark olive-green glass was typically used for champagne bottles, and their bottoms were commonly manufactured with deep basal (kick-up) indentations. Around the turn of the century, most clear glass was decolorized by adding manganese dioxide, which reacts when exposed to sunlight, turning an amethyst color (the so-called purple glass). German supplies of manganese dioxide were cut off during World War I,

FIGURE 2.33 The sizes and shapes of these bottles indicate they contained personal and medical products, including still-used products like Listerine and Vaseline. Other trademarks include "Dr. J. H. McLean's Volcanic Liniment Oil," and "KREML," a hair preparation. The tin contained quinine tablets. (Courtesy of Dames & Moore)

and thus sun-colored amethyst glass indicates sites occupied prior to World War I (although, of course, continued use and reuse for some time after that must be considered). Selenium was used as a substitute decolorizer, and some of these combinations eventually turned the glass amber (straw color) or pink, which can be used to date some containers to post–World War I times.

Other chronological information can be garnered from subtle markings related to mold seams and types of closures or lips and collars, called "finishes" because they were hand-finished prior to 1903, when Michael J. Owens invented a fully automatic bottle-blowing machine (Rock 1981); bottles with seam lines all the way to the top of the finish must postdate this invention. Different types of closures also evolved rapidly around the turn of the century as efforts were made to improve on the older cork-stopper technology. Internal screw threads were used on some whiskey bottles from the 1870s to around 1900, and continuous external threads became popular after World War I. Spring-loaded Hutchinson stoppers and lightning stoppers were common between about 1880 and 1920, especially on beer and soda bottles and canning jars. These complicated spring systems were in part replaced by the simpler crown cap, invented in 1889 and still in use today. The original cork liners were replaced with plastic around 1955.

Although glass containers are being replaced more and more by alternative types of packaging that are filling our landfills, glass bottles and jars were used and discarded extensively for a long time. Glass containers may be rather fragile, but because glass itself is so durable, it constitutes a major component of the artifactual record left for historical archaeologists to study. (Modern landfills also are being studied by archaeologists [Rathje and Murphy 1992].) Although the breaking of a bottle may destroy its beauty, the fragments can still provide considerable information for archaeologists to puzzle over and decipher.

THE ARCHAEOLOGY OF FOOD

In building the dams of central Arizona, human muscle did much of the work, and it took food to power those human engines. Much of that food came in tin cans or glass jars and bottles that became part of the archaeological record of the dam construction camps. Some of this debris was discarded near the residential areas, but much of it was hauled off to secondary dumps, a reflection of the contemporary standards of camp sanitation.

Large dumps discovered on the margins of Camp Pleasant are estimated to contain approximately 100,000 food containers discarded during the original 1926–1927 occupation and the 1934–1935 reoccupation. We suspect that similar large secondary dumps were used at the other dam construction camps but remain undiscovered, perhaps because they were buried in some remote location or inundated by the new reservoirs.

Typically, half of any assemblage of food containers from the construction camps could be identified only as having originally contained "general" foods, which most likely included a variety of vegetables and fruits (fig. 2.34). Evaporated-milk cans were almost as common, and this milk was most likely used for making foods such as biscuits, breads, and pancakes. Twenty or more specific types of food containers could be identified, but they usually represented 5 percent or less of the collections. The most common of these were containers for coffee, meat, and fish.

Collections from Camp Pleasant reflect four distinct sources of trash. A total of twenty-six food types were identified in the collections from a cluster of tent houses where about twenty to twenty-five families lived, preparing and eating their meals in tent houses. Twenty-four types were identified in the collections from the frame-house area, where supervisors and their families lived.

These numbers seem to contradict the expectation that these higher-status families might have enjoyed a somewhat more diverse diet than those living in the tent houses. However, a diversity index that accounts for differences in the sizes of the collections suggests that the frame-house families did have more diverse foods per hundred containers recovered, but only by the slightest margin. The hilltop overflow-housing area, where the lowest-status families in the camp probably resided, did yield fewer food types, and the diversity index was lower than for the two other family-residence areas.

The secondary dumps, which primarily represent mess-hall trash, yielded somewhat fewer food types than the tent-house and frame-house family areas, despite the fact that the sample collections were twice as large. Therefore, the diversity index is quite low.

In general, the collections indicate that all residents of Camp

Type of Food	Camp Pleasant Family Tents Totals	%	Frame Houses * Totals	%	Overflow Housing * Totals	%	Secondary Dumps Totals	%	Roosevelt Cement Mill Camp Totals	%	Apache Clay Quarry Camp Totals	%	Totals	%
general food	1,556	55%	1,046	48%	1,204	48%	2,056	37%	127	59%	86	79%	6,075	46%
evaporated milk	700	25%	796	36%	950	38%	3,160	58%	47	22%	0	0%	5,653	42%
keys/strips/lids	185	7%	46	2%	113	5%	66	1%	3	1%	0	0%	413	3%
meat	74	3%	99	5%	119	5%	33	1%	16	7%	16	15%	357	3%
coffee	83	3%	77	4%	42	2%	15	0%	1	0%	0	0%	218	2%
fish/salmon/kippers	43	2%	30	1%	22	1%	84	2%	4	2%	0	0%	183	1%
milk bottles	48	2%	29	1%	6	0%	11	0%	0	0%	0	0%	94	1%
baking powder	22	1%	11	1%	12	0%	5	0%	8	4%	5	5%	63	0%
lard	22	1%	4	0%	6	0%	2	0%	0	0%	0	0%	34	0%
condensed milk	14	0%	9	0%	3	0%	7	0%	1	0%	0	0%	34	0%
spices	9	0%	9	0%	6	0%	7	0%	1	0%	0	0%	32	0%
ketchup	4	0%	9	0%	5	0%	8	0%	0	0%	0	0%	26	0%
tea	13	0%	9	0%	3	0%	0	0%	0	0%	0	0%	25	0%
cocoa/chocolate	7	0%	3	0%	5	0%	4	0%	0	0%	0	0%	19	0%
syrup	4	0%	7	0%	0	0%	4	0%	1	0%	0	0%	16	0%
chili powder/chilies	2	0%	1	0%	0	0%	4	0%	6	3%	2	2%	15	0%
vinegar	9	0%	2	0%	0	0%	2	0%	0	0%	0	0%	13	0%
mayonnaise	8	0%	1	0%	2	0%	2	0%	0	0%	0	0%	13	0%
eggshell	1	0%	1	0%	0	0%	8	0%	0	0%	0	0%	10	0%
jam/jelly/preserves	3	0%	1	0%	0	0%	0	0%	0	0%	0	0%	4	0%
salt	1	0%	0	0%	0	0%	3	0%	0	0%	0	0%	4	0%
cooking oil	1	0%	1	0%	0	0%	1	0%	0	0%	0	0%	3	0%
juice	0	0%	3	0%	0	0%	0	0%	0	0%	0	0%	3	0%
pineapple	1	0%	1	0%	1	0%	0	0%	0	0%	0	0%	3	0%
peppersauce	0	0%	0	0%	0	0%	2	0%	0	0%	0	0%	2	0%
malted milk	1	0%	1	0%	0	0%	0	0%	0	0%	0	0%	2	0%
pepper	0	0%	0	0%	1	0%	0	0%	0	0%	0	0%	1	0%
Tabasco sauce	0	0%	0	0%	1	0%	0	0%	0	0%	0	0%	1	0%
olives	0	0%	0	0%	0	0%	1	0%	0	0%	0	0%	1	0%
olive oil	1	0%	0	0%	0	0%	0	0%	0	0%	0	0%	1	0%
extract	1	0%	0	0%	0	0%	0	0%	0	0%	0	0%	1	0%
Totals	2,813	100%	2,196	100%	2,501	100%	5,485	100%	215	100%	109	100%	13,319	100%
number of food types	25		24		18		22		11		4		31	
diversity index (food types/ 100 artifacts)	0.9		1.1		0.7		0.4		5.1		3.7		0.2	

* includes associated trash features

FIGURE 2.34 If we really are what we eat, these tabulations of archaeological collections recovered from Camp Pleasant, the Cement Mill camp at Roosevelt, and the Clay Quarry Apache camp at Roosevelt reveal some interesting patterns. (Courtesy of Dames & Moore)

Pleasant had similar diets. The subtle variations that were detected are consistent with variations in social status reflected in the quality of housing and access to utility systems, but the range of variation is quite narrow, suggesting that status differences were not great.

The preserved archaeological sites in the Roosevelt area did not reflect the full range of status differences found at Camp Pleasant, but some comparisons are interesting. The collection of food containers was small from the Cement Mill Camp, where eight to ten tent houses were probably occupied by relatively low-status laborers who were forced to relocate from the camping grounds on the margins of Roosevelt as it was flooded by the rising reservoir in 1908. Only eleven different food types were represented. The calculated diversity index is high in comparison to those at Camp Pleasant, but this probably reflects skewing due to the small size of the collections.

Collections from one of the Apache camps where twenty-two wickiup platforms were identified yielded only about five food containers per residence. They represented only four different food types, suggesting that the Apaches relied much less on canned and bottled foods than did other laborers.

Another factor may have skewed the Roosevelt collections. Gustav Harders (1968) indicated that tin cans were often salvaged, cut open, and flattened for use as siding and shingles on the simple residences of laborers, particularly Hispanics. If substantial numbers of tin cans were reused in this manner, this would certainly distort the patterns of the artifact collections.

Harders (1968:76) reports that "with the exception of flour, sugar, beans, and potatoes, all food came in tin cans," but those were undoubtedly substantial exceptions because such foods may have constituted a major portion of the laborers' diet. Other documents reveal that vegetables were grown locally, often by Chinese farmers. Foods that came in paper or cloth sacks, and unpackaged fresh vegetables and fruits, are unlikely to be well represented in the archaeological record, but other types of foods were represented by faunal remains.

In general, bones were not well preserved in the shallow archaeological record of the construction camps, but one pit at Roosevelt yielded almost three thousand bones. A third of these were identifiable, and of these, 59 percent were beef, 19 percent pork, and 14 percent sheep. Only a single fish bone and a single chicken bone were recovered. The origin of this trash probably was the mess hall of the temporary camp for Reclamation Service staff waiting for the facilities on Government Hill to be completed. The collections represent sides of beef from probably no more than two animals, about thirteen pigs (mostly hams), and six sheep. It appears that the government staff did not eat entirely from tin cans, and that they enjoyed at least some fresh meat supplemented with cured hams.

3

Danger

Although glamorized and mythologized within our popular culture, the Western cowboy was, in reality, a wageworker who traveled from job to job, hiring on when there was work. In their nomadic careers, dam construction workers were cowboys of construction, working in difficult and sometimes hazardous conditions, moving from construction job to construction job.

The Work

While living and working conditions at the dam construction camps were not necessarily harsh for all individuals at all times, common labor must have been difficult and demanding. Tunneling, blasting, cutting rock, mixing concrete, and grading roads, all the work of building Roosevelt Dam, used human muscle rather than heavy machinery (figs. 3.1, 3.2, 3.3, 3.4, and 3.5). For example, to avoid weakening the rock of the supporting canyon walls, workers used few explosives to excavate to bedrock and instead dug out the dam's foundation with sledgehammers, pickaxes, and shovels (Smith 1986). A contemporary description of the construction of the penstock tunnel, which fed water from the power canal to the generators in the powerhouse at the base of Roosevelt Dam, dramatizes the work. "Like the sluicing tunnel, this area was also extremely hot,

The cowboy stood tall in the saddle as the knight of the western grasslands, a folk hero idolized in literature, [but] . . . writers did not bother to represent the boredom and weariness of building and mending fences, cleaning out springs, and pulling frantic cattle from bogs. . . . Living outdoors in extremes of weather meant sandy bedrolls, tasteless or poor food, labor from daylight to dark in hazardous terrain— all this for a few dollars a month.
—BERT M. FIREMAN
(1982:166–167)

FIGURE 3.1 This February 1905 photo shows laborers constructing the High Line Road about six hundred yards west of the cement plant, above the southern abutment of the dam site. The High Line, which was built to replace portions of the road to Globe that would be flooded by the reservoir, connected with the Apache Trail at Roosevelt Dam. The Apache Trail was built to connect Roosevelt with Mesa and Phoenix. (Photograph by Walter Lubken, courtesy of the National Archives)

despite the use of an exhaust fan. Heat and gas vapors were intense" (Leighton 1906:134).

Reminiscences of the Reclamation Service doctor at Roosevelt offer another example of the physical difficulty of the work at Roosevelt. A group of rock workers from the eastern United States, mostly "double-jack" miners with experience on open quarry work, were brought in to run the "single-jack" drills needed to open the penstock tunnel. Palmer's medical department "became flooded" with forty or fifty cases of tenosynovitis of the forearm and wrist (Palmer 1979:127). The stricken men were laid off for a time until they became used to swinging four-pound hammers in one hand while holding a drill in the other.

Not all the work was done by human and animal muscle. Workers were assisted by giant mechanical devices, such as the two 1,200-foot-long cableways that spanned the canyon about 350 feet above the Salt River (Jackson 1992a). The cableways were used first to carry away the rock and gravel excavated from the foundation of the dam, and later, these same cableways carried in concrete and the huge stones—some weighing as much as ten tons—to build the dam (figs. 3.6, 3.7, and 3.8). On the dam itself, workers used the leverage of wooden stiff-arm derricks to move the stones into place (fig. 3.9). An aerial Leschen tramway, about one-third mile long, connected the cement mill and sand plant to facilitate transport of cement and aggregate to the mixing plant on the southern abutment of the dam (Smith 1908; 1909) (fig. 3.10).

FIGURE 3.2 Roosevelt workers quarry limestone in March 1905. The limestone was crushed and mixed with clay to make cement. This quarry was just uphill from the cement plant. (Photograph by Walter Lubken, courtesy of the National Archives)

An Honest Day's Pay

For two months the materials and supplies were packed in on the shoulders of men, along precipitous canyon sides, shelving rock and rolling boulders, and passed down the vertical cliffs by ladders and ropes.
—M. O. LEIGHTON
(1906:134)

Because it was isolated and without fully developed transportation and other services, the Southwest tended to be a high-wage region where it was difficult not only to attract workers, but also to keep them (Meredith 1968; Zarbin 1984). The scarcity of labor forced the Reclamation Service and contractor O'Rourke to pay sufficiently high wages to attract workers to the site. Those who were dissatisfied with the wage at Roosevelt may have taken advantage of the labor scarcity all across the West and moved on to another job.

The process of hiring laborers to work at Roosevelt seems to have been a casual one. No physical examination was required, nor were the men required to provide any references as to character and ability. Each foreman had the freedom to hire, and was instructed simply to "size him up and see if you think he can do the work." For Louis Hill, supervisory engineer for the Reclamation Service, the process was "usually the question of picking the best you can get out of a mighty poor lot" (Hill 1905:2).

Chester Smith, the senior Reclamation Service engineer for the Roosevelt project, provided comprehensive information on Roosevelt wages in a 1910 article in the *Engineering Record*, in which he described the quarrying of stone; the production of cement; the transport of mortar, concrete, and stone via two Lidgerwood cableways; and the laying of masonry. He also

FIGURE 3.3 Stonemasons square the corners of the first stone for Roosevelt Dam, September 20, 1906. (Photograph by Walter Lubken, courtesy of the National Archives)

FIGURE 3.4 All the big names at Roosevelt gathered to oversee the setting of the first stone in the dam in 1906. The caption identifies (1) L. C. Hill, U.S. Reclamation Service engineer in charge, (2) Chester Smith, Reclamation Service construction engineer, (3) J. M. O'Rourke, contractor, (4) Mr. Steinmetz, contractor, (5) John Urquehart, construction inspector, (6) Dr. R. F. Palmer, physician in charge, (7) Dr. Tim Hinchion, assistant physician, (8) Dan Carr, (9) Howard Reed, and (10) unknown. (Courtesy of the Arizona Historical Foundation)

described general repairs and detailed the labor costs for the masonry work on Roosevelt Dam during March 1909.

The most common wage for laborers at any of these tasks was $2.50 per day. The highest paid workers were four engineers at one quarry who were paid $12.00 per day, twice the amount paid to the second highest paid groups, the five foremen ($6.00 per day) and seven masons ($5.00 per day) who laid masonry on the dam using derricks to transport the stone. Others who earned high wages included the powdermen at the quarries ($4.00 and $5.00 per day) and a blacksmith at one of the quarries ($4.00 per day). Although the pay for "engineers" ranged from $2.00 to $12.00 per day, most were paid $3.50 to $4.00 per day (Smith 1910:762).

FIGURE 3.5 Not all of the stonework at Roosevelt went into the massive Roosevelt Dam. These masons, photographed in January 1904, were building a much smaller dam on Cottonwood Creek to provide potable water for the Roosevelt camps. (Photograph by Walter Lubken, courtesy of the National Archives)

FIGURE 3.6 Monstrous wooden towers supported a cableway system manufactured by the Lidgerwood Company of Chicago. The cableways were used to transport rock, concrete, and equipment to Roosevelt Dam. (Courtesy of the Salt River Project)

FIGURE 3.7 On March 8, 1906, Walter Lubken caught the cableway in action, hauling a massive piece of equipment to the Roosevelt Dam site. The cableways had a capacity of about ten tons. (Courtesy of the Salt River Project)

The historical record reveals only two incidents of discontent with wages at Roosevelt. In 1908, four Reclamation Service carpenters went on strike for higher wages and refused to work on Labor Day, September 7. Their attempts to recruit fellow workers failed because the others were happy with their eight-hour day and believed they were getting a fair wage. The four carpenters were fired, and replacements were sought in Phoenix (AR 13 Sept 1908).

A few months later, the Globe newspaper reported that many laborers had become dissatisfied with the $2.00 wage, which they felt was insufficient compared to the high cost of living at

RAISING ARIZONA'S DAMS

the dam. An unknown number of workers left the camp, and others threatened to follow their lead (ASB 20 Dec 1908).

A decade earlier, wages for workers at the 1892–1895 Camp Dyer were only slightly lower. The basic labor wage was $1.75 to $2.00 per day. Foremen earned about $.25 to $.50 more. Most skilled workers, such as carpenters, blacksmiths, engineers, stonecutters, and masons, earned $3.00 to $3.50 per day. The highest wage recorded was $4.78 per day (Maricopa County Records 1896a, 1896b, 1896c, 1896d).

In the 1920s, about fifteen years after Roosevelt Dam was completed, wages had risen somewhat. Laborers on the Lake Pleasant Dam project earned from $.30 to $.50 per hour (about $2.40 to $4.00 per day). Skilled workers such as riveters and carpenters earned $.60 to $.75 cents per hour (about $4.80 to $7.50 per day) (Imperial 1986; Horton 1986). These wages

FIGURE 3.8 The man in the derby hat, who almost certainly is photographer Walter Lubken, provides scale for this April 2, 1906, photograph of the cableway towers. Archaeological investigations discovered huge buried logs rigged as anchors to help secure these towers on their precarious hillside foundations. (Courtesy of the National Archives)

compared favorably to the national average industrial-worker wage in the mid-1920s: $.54 to $.64 cents per hour (about $4.30 to $6.40 per day) (Reisler 1976). Construction work was paying from three to five times more than agricultural work in Arizona at this time, when field workers commonly earned only about $.10 per hour.

Demand and Supply of Labor

Despite the difficult work, few dam construction workers organized into labor unions during the construction of central Arizona dams. When construction began at Roosevelt Dam, labor was in short supply—one symptom of a booming economy in a sparsely populated region—and the Reclamation Service and John O'Rourke faced a constant struggle to attract workers. Louis Hill (1905) attributed the transience of the work force to

FIGURE 3.9 By April 1910, Roosevelt Dam was nearing completion. Note the wooden derricks precariously balanced on the dam, and several others in the adjacent rock quarry. The car to the left provides a scale for gauging the massiveness of the dam. (Courtesy of the Phoenix Museum of History)

FIGURE 3.10 A Leschen aerial tramway, a system of buckets and cables almost one-third mile long, was used to carry cement from the cement mill and aggregate from the sand plant to the concrete mixing plant at the Roosevelt Dam site. (Courtesy of the Salt River Project)

the poor quality of the laborers and their lack of an appropriate work ethic.

From the laborers' perspective, they were probably voting with their feet against the less-than-ideal working conditions and the high cost of living in the remote camps, where much of their wages had to be spent for room and board. Perhaps because it was easy to find other work, there were few moves at unionization among the Roosevelt workers in contrast to contemporary labor organization in nearby mining towns such as Globe.

The shortage of labor, both skilled and unskilled, plagued the Roosevelt project throughout most of its history and led directly to efforts to recruit laborers from all ethnic and racial groups, from all over the country. A 1906 advertisement in a Globe newspaper sought two hundred laborers to work for contractor John O'Rourke at Roosevelt Dam (ASB 29 Mar 1906). A later article complained that work at the dam was "greatly retarded by the scarcity of labor" and that officials were turning to wherever they might find workers, "from Galveston to San Francisco" (ASB 28 June 1907). Italian stoneworkers were recruited from New York and Pennsylvania, Mexican laborers from El Paso, African Americans from Galveston, and Apaches from the nearby San Carlos Reservation.

There is some evidence of discontent with working conditions at Roosevelt. In 1906, a number of the African American workers brought from Texas by contractor O'Rourke found the work harder and the hours longer than they had expected, and according to a July 22 *Arizona Republican* article, they were threatening to leave "as soon as they get a payday." The article also referred to problems with other workers. "Many Italians are also employed, and the negroes do not mix well with the children of southern Europe."

The Italians had encountered their own difficulties earlier that year when "two hundred Italian workmen" employed by O'Rourke threatened to strike after a dispute between the Anglo foreman, John Conchion, and an Italian laborer. During a disagreement, Conchion struck the Italian worker across the head with a crowbar, and a rock-throwing battle ensued. Onlookers halted the struggle, but not before the Italian had to be hospitalized for stitches. He was unable to return to work the following day, and the rest of the Italian workers demanded that Conchion be removed or they would not work. After Conchion's arrest, the threatened strike was called off. Conchion pleaded guilty and paid a $6 fine (AR 23 May 1906).

Another source of discontent was the intermittent flooding at the dam site that forced work stoppages. Prevented from earning money and uncertain when work might resume, but faced with expenses of about $1 per day, many laborers would "pick up their rolls of bedding and seek employment elsewhere" (AR 5 Nov 1907). Such exoduses further depleted the already scarce supply of labor.

Despite incidents reflecting worker discontent at the Roosevelt dam site, the years of construction saw little organized protest from the workers. The single indication in the historical record of union activity at Roosevelt is the identification of John Loser, who was killed in an accident in 1908, as a member of the Globe Stonecutter's Union (ASB 26 Apr 1908). The epitaph on the gravestone erected by his fellow workers referred to Loser as "one of the unforeseen costs of the Roosevelt Dam." Given the high level of union activity among the miners of nearby Globe, the lack of reference to unions at Roosevelt is surprising (Casillas 1979; Dinnerstein, Nichols, and Reimers 1979).

Many Roosevelt workers may have shared the opinions of a carpenter employed by the Reclamation Service in the early years of construction at Roosevelt. William L. Mann told a newspaper reporter in July 1904 that he had never seen a "more gentlemanly staff of overseers" in his life. Pleased that his superiors did not make impossible demands and did not display harshness or fits of temper, Mann felt that everyone was treated "with uniform respect." "I have never," he concluded, "found a more pleasant place to work" (AR 28 June 1904).

By the Great Depression of the 1930s, demand and supply of labor had reversed, and laborers report being thankful for having jobs at places such as Bartlett Dam. Project managers at Hoover Dam, built between 1931 and 1936, worked hard to prevent unionization and were able to do so because of the labor surplus (Stevens 1988). The work force at Bartlett is reported to have been fully unionized, reflecting larger regional trends in labor organization.

Labor during the 1944–1946 construction of Horseshoe Dam was in short supply because of World War II. However, because a rockfill design was selected and much of the work for such dams had become highly mechanized, the work force may have never exceeded one hundred laborers.

Death on the Job

The enthusiastic descriptions of engineering feats accomplished during dam construction in central Arizona fail to include the cost of the dams in terms of human life and tragedy. Newspaper accounts and oral-history interviews fill in the gaps of the engineering records. A contemporary description of the construction of Roosevelt Dam paints a dramatic portrait of the work place.

> By day and by night, the dull roar of dynamite breaks the desert stillness, and the canyon walls go crashing down to furnish material for this structure. Great blocks of sandstone weighing ten tons each are swung out on cranes and set in place. When night comes, myriads of electric lights burst forth, weirdly illuminating a busy army of toilers, working gnome-like in a shadowy canyon. It is a wondrous scene, awesome, and inspiring. (Blanchard 1908:279)

However, Roosevelt proved to be a dangerous place. Approximately two dozen workers lost their lives in construction-related accidents—an average of one almost every four months. There is no documentation of the dangers at the 1892–1895 Camp Dyer, but the statistics for Roosevelt seem extraordinarily high compared to later camps. The disparity might be due to poor documentation for the other camps, or the smaller numbers of workers living in the later camps for shorter construction periods, or improved safety practices. The 1920s, 1930s, and 1940s were an era of increasing efforts to minimize unsafe working conditions at construction sites, but there still were fatalities (see "Eyewitnesses to Death," p. 114).

Two deaths at Roosevelt occurred during excavation of the sluicing tunnel. The unnamed men, probably Apache or Hispanic, apparently died because of the almost suffocating, steamlike vapor and intense heat, which rose to 130°F when hot springs were encountered (Leighton 1906; Zarbin 1984).

Within a couple of months, in October 1904, another worker died while blasting rock on the Apache Trail about fifteen miles from the dam site. Robert Schell either made a fuse on a dynamite cap too short, or he miscalculated the time he needed to escape. The resulting blast nearly blew his right arm from his shoulder and threw him thirty feet onto a rock. The unfortunate man died within hours, before a doctor summoned from Mesa could arrive (Zarbin 1984).

Two men died in the first two days of March 1905. On March 1, Alexander McGalvey died while working on the road above the dam. Workers, who often wore lifelines, were cutting twenty to sixty feet into vertical canyon cliffs (Fitch 1914). None of McGalvey's companions saw his fatal fall from a three-hundred-foot cliff to the rocks below (AR 4 Mar 1905).

The next day, Mills Van Wagenen fell to his death from the Salt River suspension bridge connecting the town of Roosevelt with O'Rourke's Camp. Van Wagenen, a twenty-year-old government employee from Globe, and three other men were watching Osborne Richins measure the flow of the river when a heavy rock broke free from the side of the mountain and crushed one of the cables holding the bridge between the canyon walls. The bridge tipped and fell twenty feet, spilling all the men except Richins into the fast-moving river. Van Wagenen, an inexperienced swimmer, was swept away; his body was found sixteen days later in some branches at the head of the Utah Canal, about forty miles downstream. The other three men who fell from the broken bridge survived (AR 8 Mar 1905; ASB 2 Mar 1905).

In addition to the deaths of Schell and McGalvey, road construction caused perhaps the most publicized death at Roosevelt. Al Sieber, a well-known former Indian scout, was working as foreman of a crew of Apache road builders when he was crushed by a stone that rolled onto the Tonto Creek wagon road. Sieber had been with the Reclamation Service since the work at Roosevelt had begun, and he was valued for his ability to supervise and communicate with Apache laborers (AR 20 Feb 1907) (see "Al Sieber," p. 115).

Several men died while working on the dam itself. During construction, giant wooden derricks balanced on top of the dam were used to swing ten-ton blocks of sandstone into place. The combination of huge stones, heavy machinery, and the great height of the dam caused at least four deaths reported in local newspapers.

In July 1907, N.J. Murphy was crushed to death when the cable snapped on an iron skip used to lower rock and concrete to the working level of the dam. An employee of contractor O'Rourke, Murphy left a wife and four children; he was buried in the Roosevelt cemetery (ASB 21 July 1907). Only a month later, J.C. Broughton was killed when the derrick he was operating toppled over and threw him thirty feet to the ground. A thirty-five-year-old native of South Carolina, Broughton had recently sent for his wife and six-year-old child in Alabama, and they were expected to arrive in Roosevelt within a few weeks (ASB 25 Aug 1907).

John Loser, the stonecutter mentioned previously, was killed the next spring when he was "crushed like a fly between the rocks and the derrick. His death was instantaneous and he presented a horrible sight when his body was reached." Apparently single and forty-five years old, he was buried in the "village cemetery" at Roosevelt (ASB 26 Apr 1908; Zarbin 1984:176).

One of the last recorded deaths during the construction of Roosevelt Dam also occurred at the top of the dam. In March 1910, a fellow worker yelled, "Look out!" to W. Dillon, a stonemason from England. Dillon turned, lost his footing, and fell more than a hundred feet from the highest point of the dam to the lake below, where he drowned. Dillon's wife and children lived in England and had not accompanied him to Roosevelt (Zarbin 1984).

At least three men died in the heavy machinery in the cement mill at Roosevelt. On Christmas Day 1907, cement-mill worker Thomas McGraw lost his footing and, in an effort to regain his balance, caught his left arm in the machinery. The arm was torn off, and he died almost immediately. No relatives could be located for the sixty-year-old former sailor, and McGraw was buried the same day (AR 3 Jan 1908; Zarbin 1984).

Less than a year later, Santiago Gomez suffered a particularly gruesome death at the cement mill. Working with two other men, Gomez had been filling buckets with cement for the dam. In an attempt to restart the cement flowing into the buckets from a large bin, Gomez was trapped in the bin under a cement flow a foot taller than he was. The unfortunate worker was buried at Roosevelt (Zarbin 1984).

Six weeks after Gomez's death, a shift foreman for the Reclamation Service was killed at the cement mill by a freak chain reaction of events. During repairs to the cement mill, the foundation for a hydraulic jack gave way, causing a large timber to hit Jesse Earl Parker. The blow toppled Parker, who fell twelve feet and fatally hit his head on a concrete floor. Sadly, his parents had just arrived for a holiday visit (AR 15 Dec 1908; ASB 16 Dec 1908).

Laborers were not the only ones to meet their deaths at Roosevelt; two managers also died. In February 1908, the head carpenter for the Reclamation Service at Roosevelt, George Greenwald, floated a raft of lumber down the Salt River with two other men. As they approached the half-finished dam, they intended to guide the raft toward the tunnel at the south end. Instead, the raft drifted too far north, into the main current of the Salt River. Two men jumped off the raft and swam to safety, but thirty-three-year-old Greenwald stayed on the raft and attempted to save the lumber. The rushing current swept the raft downriver, between the dam's northern edge and the canyon wall. Greenwald made no attempt to reach for a rope thrown from a bridge suspended between the dam and the north wall of the canyon. As the raft tipped over the stones at the downstream side of the dam, Greenwald lost his footing and drowned. The California man had been employed for several years at Roosevelt, where he had married Selma Johnson of Phoenix and had been living with her and a child (AR 12 Feb 1908, 19 Feb 1908).

One of the government's top officials at Roosevelt, engineer Almon H. Demrick, oversaw the construction of the electrical transmission line to Phoenix and often worked in dangerous situations. In September 1908, Demrick was badly injured by a gas explosion in one of the penstock tunnels. Burned and bruised, Demrick emerged from the tunnel with all of his clothes above the waist burned off except his shirt collar (AR 8 Sept 1908, 10 Sept 1908, 13 Sept 1908, 18 Oct 1908). Lightning struck twice, however, and only eight months later, in May 1909, the thirty-eight-year-old Demrick drowned during an inspection of the sluicing tunnel and gates. The gatekeeper miscalculated in opening the gates, allowing water to rush through the tunnel, sweeping Demrick to his death. The waters also swept his companion engineer through the tunnel, but A. L. Harris escaped drowning (AR 3 May 1909).

John Steinmetz, a partner in John O'Rourke's construction company, also came close to drowning in March 1906. He was thrown from his horse while crossing the river but was fortunate enough to be rescued by a workman (Zarbin 1984).

Danger at Lake Pleasant

Working conditions on the Lake Pleasant Dam and along the Beardsley Canal could be hazardous, although most documented injuries were minor, such as mashed fingers and workers stepping on nails (Maricopa County Records 1927a). A hospital at Frog Tanks treated minor injuries; those with more serious injuries were sent to a hospital in Phoenix (Imperial 1986). Oral-history informants described one worker who fell from the dam but was not seriously injured. Another worker died when a rag sticking out of his back pocket ignited as he was sitting near a barrel of gasoline (Imperial 1986; Horton 1986).

The perceived risk of different jobs in dam construction can be gleaned from a lawsuit brought against Carl Pleasant by the Home Accident Insurance Company in 1927 (Maricopa County Records 1927a). Court documents list insurance rates for twenty-three job classifications. The job classification with the highest insurance rate was "rigging" ($19.32 per $100.00 of payroll), perceived to be almost 250 times more dangerous than clerical work ($.08 per $100.00 of payroll).

Some injuries must have been more serious than mashed fingers because the suit indicates that the insurance company paid just over $6,500 in medical bills and compensation to six workers injured in October 1926. More than half of that amount was paid to a single worker, Ora Hansen, but the court documents do not detail the nature of his injuries (Maricopa County Records 1927a).

The desert environment also presented hazards. Wasp and bee stings frequently annoyed workers clearing brush for the canal, and scorpions occasionally stung workers. Rattlesnake bites were more serious, sometimes fatal; the Horton family lost a young son to a rattlesnake bite while the family was living at the dam in the 1930s (Horton 1986).

Disease in the Camps

There are no records of disease or injuries at Camp Dyer, but it seems to have been a typical camp of the times—unsanitary, dangerous, equipped with simple shelters offering little insulation from the elements, and in all likelihood, infested with fleas and lice. However, ideas of camp sanitation evolved rapidly at the turn of the century. A British doctor discovered the malaria bacillus in 1897, a Japanese researcher discovered the dysentery bacillus the following year, and in 1900, Walter Reed demonstrated that yellow fever was spread by mosquitoes. The large number of deaths among American soldiers in the Spanish-American War of 1898 was correctly attributed to inadequate or nonexistent sanitation in field camps. Subsequently, the military pioneered efforts to provide hygienic field conditions, and camp sanitation improved markedly during the 1904–1914 construction of the Panama Canal.

Employees of the Reclamation Service at Roosevelt benefited from this heightened awareness of health issues and received free medical care. Under contract to the Reclamation Service, Dr. Ralph Palmer set up a field hospital tent at Roosevelt in January 1904 with six beds and an adjoining dispensary. More than 2,200 patients sought medical treatment at the dispensary in 1904, and the hospital cared for 25 patients in the same year (AR 31 May 1905). The Reclamation Service erected a new hospital in July 1905, still canvas-covered but with a 20-patient capacity and an examining room and a treatment room. In addition to his work in the hospital at Government Hill, Palmer made weekly visits to the first aid stations at each construction camp (Palmer 1979; AR 20 Jan 1906).

Serious diseases broke out occasionally at Roosevelt. Typhoid entered Livingston in July 1904, brought into camp in raw milk supplied by a rancher on Tonto Creek. To eliminate the problem, Dr. Palmer set up a new dairy on a small pasture on the Salt River. Feverish typhoid patients were placed in canvas tarps with several inches of water and a cake of ice at the head and foot; four to six men held the sides and ends of the tarp and rolled the patient in the cool water. One man died from typhoid in the Roosevelt hospital in August 1904 (Palmer 1979) (see "Dr. Palmer," p. 117).

Smallpox was also present; a cowboy from Texas, Henry Turner, developed the disease after visiting Roosevelt in 1908

(*AR* 28 Mar 1908). The first death at O'Rourke's Camp was that of laborer Mike Mojeskowitz, who died of pneumonia in January 1906 (*AR* 1 Feb 1906).

Dental care was available only intermittently at Roosevelt. Two dentists visited the town in early 1906, one of whom might have been Tempe dentist Dr. W. G. DeVore, who "hung out his shingle for a few days" (*AR* 14 Jan 1906). Regular dental care may have been provided by amateur Jennie Lynch, who filled and extracted teeth as "her main diversion" at the dam site (*AR* 9 May 1909).

No deaths and little disease were reported for the 1928–1930 Stewart Mountain Dam construction camp, hailed as the "cleanest, neatest, most sanitary and most comfortable [camp] ever established for a big construction job." In contrast to the narrow canyons at Mormon Flat and Horse Mesa, the camp at Stewart Mountain enjoyed an "ideal" site, with daily street cleaning and trash incineration. An on-site doctor and first aid station treated injuries and illnesses at the camp, and few patients were sent to Phoenix and Mesa hospitals. Prospective employees were examined for evidence of disease or previous injury, and 20 percent of the applicants were rejected. The rationale for this process was that "when a person's physical condition is determined before he goes to work, endless ground for future claims and lawsuits is eliminated" (*AP* 1 May 1929).

The Darker Side of the West: Danger Off Duty

Isolated camps of single, male workers conjure images of rowdy, hard living, but even the incorporation of families did not eliminate all of the dysfunctional aspects of the temporary construction communities. The archaeological recovery of alcoholic beverage bottles from all camps in considerable abundance documents that drinking was a common aspect of camp life, despite the Reclamation Service ban at Roosevelt and the 1914–1933 era of Prohibition in Arizona.

The recovery of malt extract cans indicates that home brewing was widely practiced during Prohibition in places such as Camp Pleasant. Archaeologically, it is almost impossible to distinguish substance abuse from what would have been perceived as acceptable social drinking. Newspaper accounts vividly document the violent side of Roosevelt, which often involved alcohol. The employment of a sheriff and the

Until the advent of industrial work discipline, liquor was firmly ensconced in the workplace. . . . As a prop to increased performance, as a narcotic to a spent body but still active head, as a frenetic release from a world consumed by toil, liquor primed the pump of canal construction.

—PETER WAY (1993:1412)

construction of a thick-walled concrete jail testify to the dys-functional aspects of the temporary communities—which still characterize much of the American West.

Alcohol at Roosevelt

On canal construction projects in the early nineteenth century, workers not only consumed alcohol after hours but received from twelve to twenty ounces of liquor a day while on the job. The alcohol was considered part of the workers' compensation and was used both to pacify and encourage them. When asked about inebriation on the job, one former "jigger boss" an-swered, "You wouldn't expect them to work on the canal if they were sober, would you?" (Way 1993:1414).

By the early twentieth century, attitudes about the benefits of alcohol had changed as the United States headed toward Pro-hibition. Arizona was among the first states to adopt Prohibi-tion within its boundaries in 1914. During the Roosevelt proj-ect, the government banned the sale of liquor within a dry zone extending "from the sawmill to Government Wells . . . within three miles of the work" (Palmer 1979:112). To drink legally, workers had to visit saloons outside the limits of the project at Fish Creek, Mormon Flat, and Tortilla Flat on the Apache Trail, or others on the road to Globe. Although such establish-ments were too distant to be visited on a daily basis by the construction workers, they were convenient for teamsters and travelers (fig. 3.11).

Louis Hill, supervisory engineer for the Reclamation Ser-vice, worked diligently to maintain the ban. One saloon that had been in operation near the confluence of Pinto Creek and the Salt River before the dry zone was established was closed after Hill complained in 1904 that teamsters were getting drunk there, despite its location three or four miles from the nearest contractor's camp, and twelve miles from the dam (AR 29 June 1905; Salt River Project Archives 1904; U.S. Reclama-tion Service 1903–1916). Another saloon, legally located out-side the dry zone on the Globe road, about four miles from the camp at the diversion dam, was closed after an Apache died from drinking wood alcohol sold to him there (AR 8 Apr 1906; Palmer 1979).

Hill also worked with former Texas Ranger Jim Holmes to enforce the liquor ban. In 1905, Hill and Holmes stopped a stagecoach after it entered the dry zone, and they broke the four

FIGURE 3.11 These mule-drawn wagons hauled oil sixty miles from Mesa over the Apache Trail. The cement plant was operated primarily with electricity locally generated by the power canal, eliminating much of the need to import oil and greatly reducing the cost of cement. Teamsters, such as those depicted, and stage drivers also occasionally included contraband alcoholic beverages in their cargoes for the laborers living in the "dry zone" at Roosevelt. (Photograph by Walter Lubken, courtesy of the National Archives)

bottles of wine and twenty-nine bottles of whiskey they found on board. The liquor had been intended for a wedding celebration (AR 13 Oct 1905).

For a time, some of the residents drank patent medicines sold at the Roosevelt drugstore. After reading an article in the *Ladies' Home Journal* describing the alcoholic content of patent medicines, Hill banned its sale in Roosevelt (AR 28 Mar 1906). At Hill's request, Dr. Palmer took over operation of the Roosevelt drugstore, intending to eliminate the intoxicating patent medicines. After acquiring the drugstore inventory, Palmer destroyed "a couple of 50-gallon barrels of jake [an alcoholic extract of Jamaican ginger]," but he did not realize that other alcohol had been disguised as bottles of "red ink" until a customer wanted to buy two cases of it. Ranger Holmes told Palmer that this "red ink" was a favorite intoxicating drink (Palmer 1979:36–37).

Despite Hill's vigilance, workers did smuggle liquor into Roosevelt from saloons on Fish Creek and Tonto Creek. As one newspaper reporter commented, "funny what a lot of stuff is sent in by admiring friends on the outside that the recipient never orders, but generally seems to be expecting" (AR 6 June 1909). The Inn at Fish Creek was a "highly respectable and much patronized establishment with good beds, and good food. It also had a very good bar. . . . It had become the habit of the engineers in the camp to order what drinks they wanted for the weekends by calling up the Inn at Fish Creek and having it sent up on the Saturday afternoon stage" (Palmer 1979:116).

Louis Hill, Dr. Palmer, and two other men once intercepted that Saturday afternoon stage and found a case of whiskey addressed to "E. G. Lind" in the boot of the coach. The engineer who had ordered the whiskey feared that his name was unknown in camp and so had put Dr. Lind's name on the order. Hill destroyed all but two of the whiskey bottles, and allowed Lind to keep those two (Palmer 1979:118).

Although alcohol consumption was prohibited at the Roosevelt project, alcoholic beverage bottles were collected at virtually all of the Roosevelt-area sites, including Government Hill. This archaeological evidence leaves little doubt that drinking played a significant role in many of the workers' lives.

Law and Order at the Dams

Roosevelt had its share of tragedy, abuse, crime, and violence detailed in newspapers, legal records, and coroners' inquests. Although unpleasant, such stories help paint a complete and realistic picture of the workers' daily lives.

The darker side of the Roosevelt communities is perhaps best illustrated by the presence of a jail, a justice of the peace, and the Arizona Ranger Jim Holmes, who was also sheriff of Gila County (see "Ranger Holmes and the Roosevelt Jail," p. 121). The Roosevelt jail, a "ferro-concrete structure with walls, roof, and floor more than a foot thick," was completed in February 1906 (Zarbin 1984:124). A news reporter quipped that because it would be as hot as an oven in summer, would-be criminals might be hesitant to act (AR 26 Feb 1906).

Hill testified before a congressional committee in 1911 stating that alcohol had a very destructive effect on the Indian workers. He said that "Mexicans and others would give them stuff they called whiskey, and it . . . makes the Indian crazy [and] . . . an Indian when he gets drunk seems to be wild to fight." Although he recognized that "white men do the same thing with this so-called whiskey," Hill thought the Indians were affected more strongly. He recalled that when he first arrived at Roosevelt, there was a saloon near one of the camps, and if "you happened to see a man go into that saloon, in half an hour from then you would begin to hear the furniture smash" (U.S. Congress, House of Representatives 1911:640).

The reports by Anglo writers of violence among the Apaches, and between them and others, must be considered in light of the ethnocentric attitudes of the time. Articles were consistently mean-spirited, biased, and quick to place blame solely on the Indians. Still, there is little doubt that the Apaches were suffering the deterioration of their traditional culture during the construction years at Roosevelt, perhaps most obvious in the damaging effects of excessive alcohol consumption.

One of the tragedies involving an Apache at Roosevelt was the murder of Juliana Ultreras, a forty-five-year-old native of Mexico, by Gilbert Neal, an Apache. Apparently Neal had called on Ultreras at Grapevine on his way from Roosevelt to Globe to ask for something to eat. Ultreras had denied his request, called him a "son-of-a-bitch," and Neal then shot her with his rifle. Neal was apparently drinking, and he explained his actions as being the same thing a white man would do when called that name. He was found guilty and sentenced to life in prison (Gila County Records 1909; AR 17 Nov 1909).

Of course, drunkenness and violence at Roosevelt were not confined to the Apaches. In March 1906, saloon keeper Chris Gish found the body of former government employee James H. Austin, also known as "Coal Oil Jimmy," floating in the Salt River about four miles downstream from Roosevelt. Austin had apparently been visiting Gish's tent saloons outside the Reclamation Service boundaries when he was murdered by a blow to the head with a stick, after which he either fell or was thrown into the river.

Hill blamed Austin's death on the presence of the Gish saloon. Charles Walcott, the director of the U.S. Geological Service, in a letter to the secretary of the interior, compared it to the situation at another Reclamation Service effort, the

Truckee-Carson project in Nevada. Numerous murders, robberies, and other lawlessness had occurred there, Walcott claimed, because of delays in eliminating drinking establishments near the construction sites. It was always best to act quickly, he asserted, to prevent drinking, gambling, and prostitution because the proprietors were adept at delaying legal proceedings long enough to make a quick profit and move on. Hill was able to close the Gish saloon on June 4, 1906 (AR 9 Mar 1906; Gila County Records 1906a; Salt River Project Archives 1906; U.S. Reclamation Service 1903–1916).

Alcohol abuse also appears related to the disintegration of the marriage of Ellender and Earl E. Bacon of Roosevelt. In a 1909 trial, Ellender testified that her husband had abused her, called her names, struck her with his fist, and threatened and attempted to kill her with a pistol. Her husband, she lamented, was addicted to intoxicating liquors and frequently in a state of drunkenness. Although the Bacons appeared to be financially successful, owning thirteen houses and tent houses and a large number of cattle and horses, Ellender requested a divorce, custody of the children, and disposal of their property by court judgment (Gila County Records 1905–1911).

One of the most infamous murders in the area occurred in 1907 when a dam laborer, William Baldwin, raped and murdered Laura Morris, a local farmwife who baked bread for the town. He also murdered her four-year-old daughter. Baldwin was quickly apprehended by Apache trackers and Sheriff Holmes, and despite his protestations, he was taken to Globe for incarceration and trial. When a lynch mob formed and threatened to drag Baldwin from the jail, Holmes and his deputies prudently removed the prisoner through the back door. Baldwin was tried and hanged in a nearby town, Solomonville, a short time later (Hayes 1968).

Deaths also resulted from suicide and accidents associated with daily life. J. D. Chapman, an engineer from Mesa working on the derricks, shot himself with a .45 he took from one of the tents in O'Rourke's Camp. Chapman was reportedly despondent over his own and his wife's ill health (ASB 6 Dec 1908).

In a freak accident, twenty-one-year-old Mrs. Pearl Hunter of Glazier, Texas, was killed in 1906 when a small revolver fell from the pocket of a coat she was carrying over her arm and discharged a bullet that struck her in the head. Mrs. Hunter had just arrived at Roosevelt with her four-year-old daughter and was checking into her room at the boarding house at O'Rourke's Camp (Zarbin 1984).

Tragedy also befell two seven-year-old Indian children at a camp near the power canal in 1904. They were fatally burned by a brush fire while sleeping. Another child, seven-year-old Leonica Duarte, died in 1907 when kicked in the stomach by a horse. Her father, Rafael, buried the child next to an infant sister who had died only four days earlier (Zarbin 1984).

Some children were more fortunate. In 1909, the six-year-old son of M. Galez suffered only contusions and a hole through his leg when he pounded a blasting cap between two rocks. Another Mexican child, the six-year-old daughter of R. Ortiz, lost the sight in one eye and badly lacerated three fingers when she heated a .22-caliber cartridge in the flame of a lamp (AR 1 Feb 1909).

Sources of information on the construction of the Salt River Valley Water Users' Association dams on the Salt and Verde rivers are essentially silent on the darker side of camp life. A major source of information published by the association, the *Associated Arizona Producer* (later shortened to the *Arizona Producer*), described only the highlights of construction. It is known that the layout of the Stewart Mountain camp allowed the Water Users' Association to restrict entrance because all visitors had to cross the Salt River bridge at Blue Point. A camp policeman was charged with "keeping out liquor and suppressing any tendency toward rowdyism." A cattleman and former sheriff of Maricopa County, policeman Jeff Adams described his job as "the easiest job I ever had. Almost nothing for an officer to do. Sometimes I wish that someone would get obstreperous just to break the monotony" (AP 1 May 1929).

Policeman Adams' experience was not typical. Life in the West has always had elements of danger and violence, and the temporary dam construction camps of central Arizona were no exception. The project managers who hired Adams to quell "rowdyism" must have done so because they recognized the potential for violence and crime even in a relatively small, temporary community. These less pleasant aspects of social history tend to be ignored in accounts of the history of reclamation, but the history of law and order, violence, and danger has as much relevance for our modern lives as do the more typical discussions of the technology of dam building, the politics of water rights, or the economic benefits of irrigation agriculture.

Although often incomplete, eyewitness reports of fatal accidents are more moving than official reports. One account—handwritten, undated, and unsigned—was found in the Salt River Project Archives and describes early work on the Mormon Flat Dam:

> One night in August a batch of concrete plugged the steel shoot line. Two riggers went out to unplug the line. The weight of concrete caused the chains connecting the [illegible] broke. The shoots swung apart. Harry Matthews fell at once. Roy Furr in falling grabbed the edge of the shoot with one hand. He hung there for about two minutes trying to pull himself up. He fell alongside Harry, about 150 ft. drop. Harry was dead. Roy lived about two hours.

A rock slide on November 1, 1938, killed three men working on the north abutment of the Bartlett Dam, a few yards downstream of the dam. Three other men were injured. The vibrations of the jackhammers apparently loosened the rock (*Engineering News-Record*, 11 Nov 1938). An eyewitness described the tragedy in his own words (Price and Price 1986).

> I well remember when I was up on the concrete buttresses that we was building up, they was cutting rocks on the mountain to the side, and I was right level with the cliff that caved off. There was eighteen jackhammer men on it, and their helpers—nippers, we called 'em—there were about six of them. I thought it had killed 'em all. But after it fell, why, you could see one here, one there, some hanging on the ropes. It only killed three. And two of them was Indians, jackhammer men. I knew them well. It happened about five o'clock in the afternoon—I'd went to work at four.
>
> I well remember this about the excavation foreman and the superintendent—they were on the job. They tried to make the men go back to work that night. They wouldn't go back to work. The project manager, his name was Charley Clapp, pretty rough man, but fair. He sent them all home. When the midnight shift come out, he sent them all home. When the daylight shift come out, he put them on there, moving the rocks to try and make it safe.

A wayward boulder killed Al Sieber (fig. 3.12), one of the most famous men who worked on the Roosevelt project.

In February 1907, an Apache road crew was using dynamite to build the Tonto Creek wagon road just north of the dam, and one blast left a large boulder precariously balanced on a smaller stone. When Sieber, the foreman, attempted to move the boulder, he was unable to dodge out of its path, and the huge stone crushed his legs. He lost consciousness immediately and died quickly.

Sieber had been hired by the Reclamation Service because he spoke Apache fluently and could effectively supervise Apache laborers. He had honed his skills communicating with the Apaches in his twenty years as chief of scouts at San Carlos, and it is indicative of the changes in Arizona to find him as foreman for a road crew of Apache workers two decades after trailing Geronimo into Mexico, and three decades after first entering the Tonto Basin in search of gold.

In fact, Sieber's life encapsulates much of the nineteenth-century history of western America. Born in Germany in 1844, Sieber was the youngest of eight children. An older brother, John, became a political refugee in the upheavals of 1848 and convinced his widowed mother to emigrate to the United States. The family first joined a brother-in-law in Lancaster, Pennsylvania, and moved on to Minneapolis in 1856. Sieber enlisted in a Minnesota regiment in the first year of the Civil War and caught a rifle ball in his leg at Gettysburg. He was nineteen years old.

After the Civil War, in 1866, Sieber came west to San Francisco looking for work. After laying rails for the Central Pacific Railroad, he followed a silver rush to Nevada in 1867, and a gold rush to Arizona in 1868. Sieber headed to Prescott, where he found work as an assistant to mining speculator Curtis Coe Bean. (By the mid-1870s, Bean was co-owner of the rich Peck Mine in the Bradshaw Mountains, and he later served as a territorial delegate to Congress in 1884.)

In 1871, Sieber joined an expedition, led by a man auspiciously named Miner, to look for gold and silver in the Tonto Basin. The Miner expedition grew from 30 to 267 prospectors on the journey but found no precious metals. Mining continued to interest Sieber throughout his life, and he is credited with staking the first copper claim on Mingus Mountain in 1876 and filing the first gold claims in the Tonto Basin in 1879.

FIGURE 3.12 This photograph of Al Sieber on crutches with a bandaged left leg was taken in 1887 after a shoot-out with the Apache Kid, two decades before Sieber died in an accident at Roosevelt. (Courtesy of Robert Bigando)

However, Sieber's fame was not to come through gold or silver, but through his dealings with Arizona Indians. Perhaps discouraged with his failure to strike it rich in precious metals, Sieber joined the army in July 1871 as a scout under General Stoneman. Two years later, General Crook recruited Sieber to scout for Indians throughout Arizona. As chief of scouts at San Carlos between 1871 and 1891, Sieber directed Indian scouts hired by the army to locate Indian resisters, and he earned his fame by following Geronimo into Mexico on several occasions.

Just when Sieber learned to speak Apache is not clear, but his influence over the Apaches was "little short of marvelous." He was described as "a tall, well-built, fine appearing man, always well dressed. He wore long, fancy officer's boots on nearly all occasions. Absolutely unafraid and fearless [with a] strong German accent" (Barnes 1988:403). The Apaches themselves called him "Man of Iron" for his resolute courage and cleverness. While serving as chief of scouts, he suffered a bullet wound in an arm in 1875, and in 1887, his Gettysburg-wounded leg caught a second rifle ball.

After leaving the army in 1891, Sieber returned to the Tonto Basin and his mining activities, filing additional claims in 1895, 1896, and 1899 (LeCount 1976), but the Reclamation Service hired him away from his prospecting to direct a crew of Apache road workers. In his early sixties and limping from the two old rifle wounds to his leg, Sieber could not escape the rolling boulder on the Tonto Creek wagon road that February day.

Sieber's life is commemorated by a monument in the Globe cemetery where he is buried. A second monument north of Roosevelt Dam along the Tonto Creek road, paid for by the Apache work crew, commemorates his death. Asked once about his influence with the Apaches, Sieber attributed his success to a simple philosophy: "I do not deceive them but always tell them the truth. When I tell them I am going to kill them, I do it, and when I tell them I am their friend, they know it" (Barnes 1988:403).

DR. PALMER

Just as Al Sieber's life encapsulated many of the themes of nineteenth-century history—the Civil War, Western gold rushes, and Indian campaigns—the life of Ralph Palmer (fig. 3.13) reflected several twentieth-century Arizona themes: health seekers, water control, and urban growth. Thirty years younger than Sieber, Palmer came to Roosevelt as a young doctor to serve as the project's chief surgeon. During his years in Arizona, Palmer was acquainted with nineteenth-century personages such as Sieber, rancher Corydon Cooley of Show Low, and homesteaders like the Goodfellows of Tonto Natural Bridge and the Schneblys of Sedona, and he also worked with twentieth-century figures such as Dr. A. J. Chandler, Governor B. B. Moeur, and Theodore Roosevelt.

Born in Michigan in 1875, Ralph Fleetwood Palmer spent four years at the University of Michigan and four more years in medical training, graduating from Cook County Hospital in Chicago in June 1902. After graduation, Palmer came to Arizona to clear up a persistent sinus infection and to visit his tubercular brother. Dr. Palmer took the territorial medical licensing exam in July 1902 and became the forty-third registered physician in the Arizona Territory.

For about four months, he practiced in Prescott, but he found the town of two thousand had "some fifteen other doctors. As the most recent arrival, my practice did not boom immediately." Palmer had "$13.00 in the bank and 50 cents in [his] pocket" when he heard that a doctor in Camp Verde wanted to sell his practice. Borrowing from a friend, Palmer paid the doctor $100.00 down, putting the remaining $300.00 on a note (Palmer 1979:16–20).

The doctor's practice included a few drugs, a cow, and a horse. About the same time, towards the end of 1902, Palmer bought the entire stock of a closed drugstore in Prescott from the druggist's widow for $25.00 cash. Thus, when he established his new practice in Camp Verde in January 1903, Dr. Palmer also set up the settlement's first drugstore.

The "usual medical fees in Arizona in those days were $3.00 [for] office visits, $5.00 [for] home visits plus $1.00 per mile one way." Many patients lived twenty-five to seventy-five miles from Camp Verde, and if the doctor stayed on a day or two to nurse the patient, as was often the case, the fee was $25.00 a day. In comparison, Al Sieber was paid $2.50 per day as foreman of a road crew at Roosevelt in 1905. Of course, patients often paid Dr. Palmer in chicken eggs and horses, and some never paid at all. But at the end of a year in Camp Verde, Dr. Palmer owned four horses, six mules, and three wagons; had paid the $300.00 he owed on the note for his practice; and still had some $2,000.00 in cash (Palmer 1979:67–68).

Palmer's job as chief surgeon at Roosevelt came about as such opportunities often do, through a friend of a friend. Archie Harris, after receiving an appointment as engineer on the Roosevelt project, contacted his college friend Harold Treadway, and Treadway referred Harris's questions about Arizona to his college friend Ralph Palmer. While Harris lived in the new settlement of Livingston, Mrs. Harris, a tuberculosis patient, stayed with the Palmers in Camp Verde. On a visit to his wife, Harris described the dam project to Palmer and suggested that he apply for the job. Dr. and Mrs. Palmer packed their belongings and moved to Roosevelt in January 1904. Supervisory engineer Louis Hill later told Palmer that he had been chosen for his medical qualifications and because all of the forty-nine other applications suggested political influence.

At Roosevelt, Dr. Palmer received $1.00 per man per month,

FIGURE 3.13 Ralph Palmer, a decidedly twentieth-century doctor and businessman, worked at Roosevelt alongside the Indian scout Al Sieber, a decidedly nineteenth-century character. (Courtesy of the Mesa Historical Society)

and that payment was to cover all professional services, including hospitalization, medicines, and dressings. In his autobiography, Palmer noted that "while the contractors' camp provided the usual number of fractures and minor accidents, there was almost no sickness among the employees" (Palmer 1979:127).

Dr. Palmer set up first aid stations in each of the work camps, and visited each station once a week. The round trip totaled about two hundred miles as he rode from the road-building camps on the Apache Trail west of Roosevelt Dam to the sawmill camp in the Sierra Ancha Mountains, north and east of the dam. Dr. Palmer treated private patients as well as Reclamation Service employees, and he also pulled teeth and did autopsies.

An intelligent and caring man, Dr. Palmer assumed duties that ranged far beyond healing the sick. He assisted with the layout of the Reclamation Service camp and helped construct a water-transport system that supplied spring water to Government Hill, Newtown, and O'Rourke's Camp. Dr. Palmer also concerned himself with sanitation at Government Hill, where he and his wife and daughters lived. After an outbreak of typhoid in the summer of 1904 that was suspected to have come from infected milk, Dr. Palmer started a new dairy with partner Charley Hill. Palmer also supervised the daily inspection and liming of the latrines that were used during the first years at Roosevelt. Later, he supervised the installation of a septic tank system for the residents of Government Hill.

Not only did Palmer broaden his experience and expand his professional practice while living at Roosevelt, but he and his wife also began to raise a family. Betty Palmer was the first baby born at the Roosevelt project, in March 1904. Another daughter, Harriet, followed. In 1906, Dr. Palmer left Roosevelt and moved his family to Mesa, where he set up a private practice, but he continued to work for the Salt River Valley Waters Users' Association as well.

In 1907, Palmer opened the first hospital in Mesa, which was simply a rented house with a capacity for only three patients. A few years later, he spearheaded a $10,000 fund-raising drive to build the Southside District Hospital at Main and Hibbert. This fourteen-bed facility was fully equipped with examination and treatment offices and an operating room (AR 18 Dec 1954; Palmer 1979:150–152).

However, Ralph Palmer, who was also a registered pharmacist, was not content building hospitals, and he also opened a number of drugstores. After his first drugstore in Camp Verde, Dr. Palmer bought the Roosevelt drugstore in 1905, a drugstore on South MacDonald in Mesa about 1906, Everybody's Drug Store on the corner of MacDonald and Main in 1908 (the building remains a drugstore today), and the Crescent Drug Store in the 1920s, also in Mesa. Palmer also built the Tempe Court, a group of twenty-eight bungalows for winter visitors.

When President and Mrs. Theodore Roosevelt came to dedicate the dam in March 1911, Dr. Palmer treated Teddy's severe laryngitis by spraying his throat with a solution of cocaine and adrenalin. Palmer's laconic comment was, "I also had the privilege of treating an ingrown toenail for Mrs. Roosevelt, so there are compensations for practicing in out of the way places" (Palmer 1979:129).

While in Mesa, Palmer worked to establish many of the institutions of a "big city." He was the first president of the Mesa Rotary Club, was elected mayor of Mesa (1910–1912), served as a vestryman at St. Mark's Episcopal Church, and helped build the Shrine Temple in Phoenix. From 1933 to 1939, Governor (and doctor) B. B. Moeur appointed Palmer to the Arizona Industrial Commission. Palmer returned to private practice until his semiretirement in 1950, at seventy-five years of age. He died four years later, a week before Christmas 1954.

When the Roosevelt Dam project began, the federal government banned liquor within a three-mile radius of all construction facilities and camps. To enforce this prohibition, supervisory engineer Louis Hill hired a former Texas Ranger named Jim Holmes to control the sale and consumption of alcohol within the project area. He, in turn, hired at least two deputies.

Holmes carried two .38 Colt automatics and could keep a tomato can "in the air shooting alternately from right and left hips until there was nothing left of the can or both guns were empty" (Zarbin 1984:115). Holmes quickly established a reputation for being all too willing to use his pistols to ensure the peace. In his autobiography, Dr. Ralph Palmer (1979:112), chief surgeon at Roosevelt Dam, recalled Jim as a "small, wiry, blue-eyed Dane" who "shot first" and asked questions later.

Two men died at Roosevelt as a result of Holmes's quick temper and excellent aim. L. Abriso, described as a Mexican bootlegger, was daring enough to attempt an escape while being escorted to jail. When Abriso shot Holmes's deputy in the arm, Holmes turned and planted five bullets in his prisoner. Dr. Palmer examined the body and found "one [bullet] in the forehead, one in the neck, one in the chest and two in the abdomen" (Palmer 1979:113).

A year later, in 1906, local papers reported that a group of Apache men under the influence of liquor had begun fighting.

FIGURE 3.14 The solid, windowless, reinforced-concrete construction of the Roosevelt jail contrasts with the typical tent housing and symbolizes efforts devoted to maintaining law and order in the camps. (Courtesy of the National Archives)

The fight resulted in two men being severely cut, and a woman being shot in the leg. Sheriff Holmes and Constable Davis were called to restore order in the camp (*AR* 23 Feb 1906; *ASB* 22 Feb 1906). A few days later, under controversial circumstances, Sheriff Holmes killed a fifty-year-old Indian, Matze, by shooting the man five times. The *Arizona Republican* described the incident as the "latest" death of an Indian because of "too great a love for native drink." "All" of the Indians living in Cottonwood Canyon "went on a spree" drinking their native corn beer, and "as usual," after a few hours of drinking, the men became abusive and began attacking women. Two of the women went to Holmes for assistance and were able to induce Holmes and Constable Fred Russell to go to the camp. Holmes testified that when he reached the camp, he saw a man sitting on a wagon, raising a .44 Winchester as if to shoot. Holmes responded by shooting the Indian five times. Holmes stated that when he picked up the Indian's weapon, it was cocked with one shell in the chamber and seven in the magazine. The jury found that Holmes had acted correctly.

However, Indians who testified at the inquest did not agree with either Holmes or the reporter. According to them, Holmes killed the wrong man (Matze), then handcuffed the appropriate individual ("S.B. 24"), and took him away. They also testified that dead Matze had not been angry or drunk, had posed no threat, had received no warning from Holmes, and had been shot three times after falling to the ground (Gila County Records 1906b). Dr. Palmer, who examined the body before it was buried at the "Indian graveyard," recalled that the holes in the Indian were within a "fraction of an inch in the same location as the five holes in the Mexican bootlegger, so there was no question as to the author" (Palmer 1979:114).

If fear of Holmes's retribution was not enough to tame the wildest would-be offender, anxiety over the thought of being locked up in the Roosevelt jail might have been (fig. 3.14). The jail was solid, sweltering, and held no hope of escape. Archaeological evidence confirms that the entire building was made of reinforced concrete about a foot thick, and during the summer months, the concrete box must have felt like an oven to anyone foolish enough to risk incarceration.

4

Discrimination

The United States is commonly said to be a "melting pot" in which diverse ethnic groups have blended to create a new democratic culture blessed with amazing hybrid vigor. The term is relatively new, first appearing in *Webster's Dictionary* in 1934 (Rabinowitz 1983). Although the credo of "equal opportunity for all" dates from the founding of our country, the reality is that ethnic labels, and the stereotypes that went with them, were a routine aspect of daily life—and still are (see "Ethnic Labels and Stereotypes," p. 150). Historians have come to realize, somewhat belatedly, that one of the unique characteristics of the American West is the multitude of diverse ethnic groups who immigrated from around the globe and converged in a relatively short span of time to create a new society that we are still trying to come to terms with.

From today's perspective, the two-dimensional portrayal of "cowboys versus Indians" that dominated public perceptions of the West for so long seems to be such a gross oversimplification that we can hardly imagine moviegoers or novel-readers ever accepting that image as anything close to reality. We also have come to realize that the more academic "frontier model" of American expansion (Turner 1985), which dominated historical perspective for almost a century, and the model's accompanying portrayal of an unpopulated region where men could determine their own destinies also are myopic. Even in the wide-open American West, who individuals were, or were able

As was true throughout the West, there was much more to the racial, religious and ethnic mix of people in Arizona than was suggested by the White Anglo cowboy, who, in fact, was often neither White nor Anglo, and the too simplistic American Indian imagery.
—PHYLIS MARTINELLI and
LEONARD GORDON
(1992:69)

to become, always was influenced greatly by their racial origin or country of birth.

The workers at the Dyer Diversion Dam went unpaid when work was abandoned in October 1895. Court records list 126 laborers by name, providing some clues regarding the ethnicity of the work force. Admittedly, names can be misleading, but they suggest that out of every ten workers, about six were Anglo, three were Hispanic, and one was Italian (Maricopa County Records 1896a, 1896b, 1896c, 1896d). One of the laborers was African American (see "Jerry Jones," p. 151).

The federal census of 1910 was taken after the Roosevelt Dam work force had peaked, but nevertheless it provides the best insight into the ethnic diversity of the historic dam construction communities of central Arizona. The census counts were tallied in three districts, documenting substantial ethnic variation among the construction camps (fig. 4.1).

In 1910, 164 residents were counted on Government Hill. The census confirms that the Reclamation Service staff, living on the hill, had the fewest minorities of any of the camps. Almost four out of five were U.S.-born whites. Half of the 34 immigrants living in the headquarters camp were Italian, and the other half included men born in Germany, Scotland, England, French Canada, Japan, and China. Congressional authorization for the Roosevelt Dam project specifically precluded the hiring of "Mongolians" as laborers (Newell 1904:82; U.S. Reclamation Service 1902–1919), but a few Asians were employed on Government Hill to work in the mess hall or hospital, or perhaps as domestics (see "Chinese Liquor Bottles," p. 153). One African American, a hospital orderly, also lived on Government Hill, but no Mexicans or Mexican Americans lived in the headquarters camp.

O'Rourke's Camp had 190 residents in 1910, less than half its peak population of more than 400 a couple of years earlier (Hantman and McKenna 1985). Nearly one of every two residents was an immigrant, and one-third of the immigrants were Spaniards—a disproportionately high number considering that Spanish immigrants made up only 0.1 to 0.2 percent of the country's foreign-born population (U.S. Bureau of the Census 1913)—perhaps reflecting some targeted labor recruiting. Almost a third of O'Rourke's immigrants were Italians, and a fifth were from central Europe. There also were six Mexican and five Chinese immigrants. More than one in ten of the residents were African Americans, most of whom were apparently recruited from Galveston, Texas, where they had worked for O'Rourke constructing a seawall (Zarbin 1984).

In Newtown, there were 287 individuals in 1910, also a decline from the peak construction period. Only about a third of the residents were whites born in the United States. Although most of the business owners in Roosevelt were whites of Euro-American heritage, Newtown was dominated by Mexicans, Mexican Americans, and American Indians (fig. 4.2). A few Chinese and Mexicans ran restaurants in this entrepreneurial town, which became home for many lower-status members of the construction community.

Although the 1910 census taker counted only sixty-six Indians in Roosevelt, bits of historic documentation suggest that hundreds of Apaches were living in the area. Archaeological research resulted in the discovery of several historically undocumented camps where Apache laborers and their families resided, strongly suggesting that a fourth census district, distinctly Apache, should have been defined.

Separate but Not Equal

According to the 1910 Roosevelt census, ethnic groups tended to be segregated among the different camps of the construction community. There also is some indication that living quarters within individual camps were segregated along lines of race, ethnicity, and class or social status. Within O'Rourke's Camp, Italians, Spaniards, African Americans, and other groups apparently clustered into distinctly ethnic neighborhoods. The Chinese-owned restaurant in Roosevelt is said to have been the only one that would serve Apaches.

Other indications of segregation were more blatant. At the Granite Reef Diversion Dam camp north of Mesa, the mess hall was Y-shaped, with separate arms for Mexicans and whites (Brown 1978). The plan of the bathhouse for the 1928–1930 Stewart Mountain camp was designed with separate "American" and "Mexican" sections. A map of the 1936–1939 Bartlett Dam camp identified a separate area, beyond the formally planned camp for government and construction contractor employees, as an "Indian Camp."

At the time, such segregation was not uncommon. For example, the Reclamation Service camp at Elephant Butte Dam in New Mexico had "Mexican quarters" in "Lower Town" while engineers and office personnel lived in "Upper Town" (Boyd and Etchieson 1986). A 1910 map of the Reclamation Service camp at the Belle Fourche Dam in South Dakota identified distinct "Bulgarian Quarters" (Ready 1910). The 1910 construction camp along the Catskill Aqueduct in New York

The physical proximity of people does not ensure communities; human relationships create communities.

—RICHARD WHITE
(1991:298)

had an "American Barracks," an "Italian Camp," and a "Negro Camp" (*Engineering Record* 1910).

Today, ethnic and racial segregation is regarded as blatantly discriminatory, but how segregation was perceived historically is not well documented. Some people may very well have resided with others of their own ethnic group for the comfort of familiar language and customs, but they undoubtedly faced other barriers imposed by the dominant society.

Residential segregation also carried over into the dam construction work at Roosevelt, where supervisors often formed work crews along ethnic lines, perhaps to avoid intercultural friction and to minimize language barriers. For example, Apaches worked together in labor crews, particularly for building roads (fig. 4.3). Many laborers of Mexican heritage worked at chopping wood or freighting supplies (figs. 4.4 and 4.5). The African Americans and Italians recruited by O'Rourke worked

ETHNICITY BY GENDER AND AGE AT ROOSEVELT, 1910

Ethnicity	O'Rourke's Camp				Government Hill				Newtown				Total			
	M	F	C	Total	M	F	C	Total	M	F	C	Total	M	F	C	Total
U.S. Born																
White	50	19	11	**80**	63	33	32	**128**	30	21	48	**99**	143	73	91	**307**
Mexican-American	0	0	0	**0**	0	0	0	**0**	45	11	21	**77**	45	11	21	**77**
Indian	0	0	0	**0**	0	0	0	**0**	18	11	37	**66**	18	11	37	**66**
Black	11	4	5	**20**	1	0	0	**1**	0	0	0	**0**	12	4	5	**21**
Chinese	3	0	0	**3**	1	0	0	**1**	0	0	0	**0**	4	0	0	**4**
Subtotal	64	23	16	**103**	65	33	32	**130**	93	43	106	**242**	222	99	154	**475**
Foreign Born																
Mexico	6	0	0	**6**	0	0	0	**0**	11	13	17	**41**	17	13	17	**47**
Italy	24	1	1	**26**	8	3	6	**17**	0	0	0	**0**	32	4	7	**43**
Spain	29	0	0	**29**	0	0	0	**0**	0	0	0	**0**	29	0	0	**29**
Central Europe	17	0	0	**17**	0	0	0	**0**	0	0	0	**0**	17	0	0	**17**
China	5	0	0	**5**	2	0	0	**2**	1	0	0	**1**	8	0	0	**8**
Germany	1	0	0	**1**	3	0	0	**3**	1	0	0	**1**	5	0	0	**5**
Japan	0	0	0	**0**	4	0	0	**4**	0	0	0	**0**	4	0	0	**4**
Scotland	1	0	0	**1**	3	0	0	**3**	0	0	0	**0**	4	0	0	**4**
Ireland	1	0	0	**1**	0	0	0	**0**	2	0	0	**2**	3	0	0	**3**
England	0	0	0	**0**	3	0	0	**3**	0	0	0	**0**	3	0	0	**3**
French Canada	0	0	0	**0**	2	0	0	**2**	0	0	0	**0**	2	0	0	**2**
Denmark	1	0	0	**1**	0	0	0	**0**	0	0	0	**0**	1	0	0	**1**
Subtotal	85	1	1	**87**	25	3	6	**34**	15	13	17	**45**	125	17	24	**166**
Total	149	24	17	**190**	90	36	38	**164**	108	56	123	**287**	347	116	178	**641**

M = males; F = females; C = children

Source: U.S. Department of Commerce and Labor, Bureau of the Census, Thirteenth Census: 1910-Population, Manuscript Population Schedule for Gila County, Arizona.

FIGURE 4.1 These census counts were made after the peak of construction, but they provide the best demographic information of any of the temporary dam construction communities that were studied. However, archaeological evidence and other historical clues indicate that the Apache population was much larger than that counted by the census taker. (Courtesy of Dames & Moore)

FIGURE 4.2 The caption for this 1908 photograph identifies the women and children in front of a Roosevelt store as Mexicans. (Courtesy of the Arizona Historical Foundation)

on the dam and adjacent quarries, but apparently in separate crews most of the time (fig. 4.6).

Local tradition maintains that most Italians were skilled stonemasons, and in fact, eight of the ten stonemasons or stone-cutters listed in the 1910 census were Italian. However, other evidence reveals that some of the stonemasons were from Scot-land, Germany, and Switzerland, and many Italians worked as unskilled laborers. Because of the ban against "Mongolian" labor, many of the Asians worked in food and laundry services, and others sold produce from their gardens.

This ethnic division of labor led to a form of discrimination that still characterizes our modern society—unequal access to higher-paying jobs. Historical documents indicate that a few Apaches were employed as subforemen for the Apache road crews, and one newspaper article refers to a "Mexican boss" at one of the clay quarries (AR 18 Dec 1908). However, most of the supervisors, engineers, surveyors, doctors, lawmen, electri-cians, carpenters, construction inspectors, and store owners were whites of Euro-American ancestry.

Rarely are the lives of laborers well documented by historic records, and with only a few exceptions, we know little of how

FIGURE 4.3 The Apache workers at Roosevelt are particularly remembered for building the Apache Trail, cut through the Salt River canyon from Roosevelt to Mesa, a distance of sixty miles. This Apache worker, photographed on June 14, 1906, is shown with a team and scraper, tools that would have been used for road work, but when photographed by Walter Lubken, he was excavating the power canal about four miles upstream of Livingston. (Courtesy of the Salt River Project)

FIGURE 4.4 These bags of cement produced at the Roosevelt mill prominently display the Reclamation Service acronym. Although ambiguous, the laborers in this circa 1907 photograph appear to be Hispanic or another ethnic minority, and their style of dress contrasts with that of the white supervisor on the left. (Courtesy of the Salt River Project)

FIGURE 4.5 Mexican men often worked as teamsters hauling supplies to Roosevelt. Walter Lubken photographed this pack train in July 1904 on the trail between Goldfield and Mormon Flat. (Courtesy of the National Archives)

the dam construction experience affected the lives of individual workers (see "Dam Builders: Some Individual Stories," p. 155). If true to the broader patterns of the West, few laborers who started out in bottom-tier jobs were able to become upwardly mobile (White 1991). "Pulling yourself up by your bootstraps" proved to be a myth for most wageworkers in the West.

Although other historians have commonly found evidence throughout the West for a "Mexican wage" or a "Chinese wage," indicating unequal pay for equal work, there is limited evidence of this type of discrimination in the dam construction camps of central Arizona. Some white workers classified as unskilled laborers at the 1892–1895 Camp Dyer earned about 15 percent more ($2.00 as opposed to $1.75 per day) than other white laborers and all of the workers with Hispanic and Italian names. Perhaps there were legitimate reasons for different wages, but they are undocumented, and the pattern is suspicious. The historical record at Roosevelt emphasizes the Reclamation Service's conscientious policy of paying even the Apache laborers the standard $2.00 per day, which was comparable to what other unskilled laborers were paid.

The motivation for the Reclamation Service's policy of equal pay for equal work is not well documented. Labor throughout the West was in short supply at the time, and the Reclamation Service was desperate for a good work force. The Apaches, in effect, came to the rescue of the Reclamation Service when they became wageworkers at Roosevelt. Within the complex ethnic milieu of the Roosevelt construction community, the story of the Apaches stands out as a paradox.

The Apache Experience at Roosevelt

Some sixty miles east of Phoenix, the federal engineers found a wild, rugged gorge where they could construct a gigantic storage dam . . . the workers who erected it were unmistakably southwestern Americans: a crew of Apaches, not twenty years removed from Geronimo's warrior bands, with a scattering of local Hispanics and of Anglo hoboes recruited from farms and freight cars.
—DONALD WORSTER
(1985:172–173)

On March 18, 1911, Theodore Roosevelt was in Arizona to dedicate the dam that bears his name. Before the formal ceremony, the powerfully built former president, wearing a black coat and khaki pants tucked into leather leggings, strode across the enormous dam accompanied by the territorial governor of Arizona, Reclamation Service officials, prominent local officials, and many former Rough Riders who had served under Roosevelt in the Spanish-American War. (Three-fourths of the Rough Riders [First U.S. Cavalry Volunteers] had been recruited from Arizona and New Mexico, and Roosevelt Dam was promoted, in part, as a reward for their service [Zarbin 1984].) A contingent of thirty Apache laborers was almost lost in the crowd, but Roosevelt paused before a banner that read "Apaches Helped Build Roosevelt Dam," and he shook hands with several of them, expressed his thanks for their efforts, and presented them with awards.

Historians have generally acknowledged that Apaches were involved in building Roosevelt Dam, but the extent of their contribution and its effect on their culture have never been thoroughly probed. The historical records are often silent about the Apaches at Roosevelt. For example, virtually none of their camps were plotted on any of the project maps, and although the Reclamation Service's staff photographer took hundreds of photographs, including a series of Apaches in "noble savage" poses, only a handful actually show Apache laborers at work.

The popular press seems to have been intrigued with the thought of Apaches working for wages, but the reality was apparently not enough for most reporters, who resorted to romantic or paternalistic images. "Where Geronimo's blood-

FIGURE 4.6 These African American workers were photographed on September 7, 1906, shoveling mud and debris from the foundation of Roosevelt Dam. (Courtesy of the National Archives)

thirsty band once spilt blood, his followers now help the white man make the desert bloom," reads one account (Steele 1918). In the early 1900s, the reference to Geronimo was still a fresh one.

Pre-Roosevelt Days: A Disintegrating Culture

The Apache groups in the Southwest (along with the Navajo) speak an Athapaskan language that marks them as immigrants from northern Canada (Perry 1991). The chronology and route of their migration before the dawn of historic records is a subject of active research and debate, but these Athapaskan speakers are clearly newcomers compared to the Hopis, Pimas, and Yavapais. When supervisory engineer Hill of Roosevelt Dam hired Apache laborers to work on the project in 1903, the

Apaches may have been in the Southwest for perhaps four or five hundred years, but only seventeen years had passed since the close of the lengthy conflict called the Apache wars.

From before the Civil War until 1886, Apache warriors had fought sporadically with the most-recent immigrants to Arizona, the white settlers and the U.S. Army units sent to defend the territory. Although there had been intermittent clashes for 150 years between Apaches and other Indians, Apaches and Spaniards, Apaches and Mexicans, and Apaches and American settlers, the final round of conflict was ignited when Lieutenant George Bascom mistakenly accused the Apache leader Cochise of kidnapping a child during a raid on a southern Arizona ranch in 1861. (Another Apache band had taken the youngster.) After years of conflict, Cochise yielded, and most Apaches moved onto reservations. From time to time, however, renegade bands roamed beyond the reservations and continued their raids in Arizona and, occasionally, Mexico. Apache resistance finally was broken in 1886, when Geronimo, the last great Apache leader, agreed to terms and surrendered (Spicer 1962).

Life on the reservation may have proved to be more destructive to the Apaches than armed conflict. U.S. Indian agents sought to suppress Apache customs and religious beliefs and to bend the Apaches to the ways of the white culture. The Apaches traditionally migrated across vast hunting and harvesting grounds with the changing seasons, and the area where Roosevelt Dam was built had been the territory of the Pinal and Tonto bands of the Western Apache. The new reservations greatly restricted their horizons.

As seminomadic hunters and gatherers, Apaches did not accumulate great stores of surplus goods. Food-producing chores were shared by adults in multigenerational extended families. Nuclear families, called *gowa*, were composed of a woman, her husband, and their children. Each gowa lived in a single wickiup unless the family was exceptionally large (fig. 4.7). Related nuclear families usually erected their wickiups near each other to form extended family groupings called *gota*. Clusters of gota, related by clan ties or marriage, formed camps called *itakowa*, headed by a *nuxwagoya hi*, the "smart one," or leader. Women worked together to gather wild foods and occasionally garden, while men typically hunted in twos and threes. Individuals who collected or hunted on their own were considered selfish and antisocial (Adams 1971).

Ethnographer Grenville Goodwin, who spent years among the Apaches in the 1930s, described their ethic of community as one in which "often the unfortunate were carried along by the fortunate, the unskilled by the skilled, the lazy by the industrious" (Goodwin 1942:123). Sharing and cooperation among relatives were keystones of Apache culture, and it was important to have "lots of relatives" (Cutter 1987).

When the Apaches were deprived of their traditional means of gathering food, their traditional sense of community and personal values suffered. Increasing reliance on nontraditional foods rationed by the Office of Indian Affairs—wheat flour, sugar, and coffee—plus the widespread pressures of poverty and joblessness on the reservations created friction between the different bands, confined in uncharacteristically restricted territories. Some of the Apaches turned in frustration to alcohol, and there were incidents of domestic violence and other evidence that the fabric of Apache culture was threatened (Goodwin 1935).

As the nineteenth century came to an end, the Apache culture was in steep decline. They had suffered under the whims of the evolving federal policy that had sought to solve the "Indian problem" first by exterminating them, and then by subjugating

FIGURE 4.7 Walter Lubken wrote his own description of this January 1908 photograph: "The Apache and her home [a wickiup]. Approaching the Indian camp the squaw can be seen coming out with a basket for sale, naturally supposing that the visitors are looking for baskets. When the camera is flashed before their eyes there is war at once as they do not like to be photographed." (Courtesy of the National Archives)

them. Many people believed the Indians could be made into peaceful subordinates by turning them into farmers or ranchers and placing them on segregated reserves. Then the Office of Indian Affairs adopted a policy of integrating Indians into the regional work force as wage laborers. "Our first duty to the Indian is to get him off the reservation and to teach him to work," the Indian commissioner proclaimed in 1906 (Hoxie 1973:165–244).

The Apaches of the San Carlos Reservation in eastern Arizona were told to cut their hair and wear hats and dungarees instead of traditional clothing. Some took jobs chopping wood, driving cattle, making adobe, grading roads, working on railroad gangs, or working in the expanding copper mining industry. Others were offered more distant work in the beet fields of Colorado or on the levees along the Colorado River near Yuma, but provisions were rarely made for the families of the laborers, whom they were very reluctant to leave behind.

The Apaches earned a reputation as hard workers, but they were judged to be unreliable because they often worked only until their immediate needs were met. Then they would disappear, only to report for work again weeks later with no explanation. Often such absences were due to family or clan obligations, which were of paramount importance to the Apaches. As a part of promoting the new policy of wagework, food rationing at the San Carlos Reservation was halted in June 1902, the same month that Theodore Roosevelt signed the Reclamation Act into law (U.S. Department of the Interior 1902).

According to supervisory engineer Hill, the San Carlos Apaches approached him to appeal for jobs as work began on Roosevelt Dam. The cutting off of rations may have stimulated the Apaches to seek such work, but it is well documented that Hill was having a hard time recruiting laborers to work at the remote dam site. However it happened, Hill hired them, and during the dam construction era, perhaps as many as 1,500 Apache laborers and their families lived in camps in the Roosevelt area. The San Carlos Reservation, home to 2,275 people prior to 1903, was reported to be so depopulated that the local Indian agent had to hire Mexicans to maintain the agency's farm (U.S. Department of the Interior 1904).

Reading the Wickiups

Despite the number of Apaches who lived at Roosevelt during the dam construction era, historical documents reveal little of their experience there. Where had they lived? Under what circumstances? When historical archaeological studies were initiated in 1986, serendipity played a significant role in shedding light on the story of the Apache laborers.

While surveying a highway realignment for a new bridge upstream from Roosevelt Dam, archaeologists found what came to be recognized as Apache artifacts. The initial clues were enamelware pots, pans, bowls, and wash basins that had been punctured with knives or axes, or otherwise rendered unusable (fig. 4.8). In a leap of "ah ha!" intuition, archaeologists hypothesized that these destroyed artifacts were personal possessions that had been ritually "killed" in conjunction with traditional Apache mortuary customs.

When an Apache died, friends and relatives buried some of the deceased's personal possessions in the grave or ritually destroyed other goods (Haley 1981; Perry 1972). If the person died inside a wickiup, the dwelling was burned along with any perishable belongings, and sometimes the area was abandoned. The deceased's horse often was killed. The destructive ritual killing was intended to clearly demarcate the worlds of the living and the dead.

The logic was multifaceted. First, Apaches believed that the destroyed goods could be used by the deceased in the afterlife. Second, Apaches feared the ghosts of the dead might return to punish anyone who used their possessions. Third, if a person were to use the possessions of the deceased, it could be construed as purposeful longing for the death of another tribal member—a horrible thought to Apaches. Fourth, Apaches preferred to eliminate objects that would remind them of the death so as to not prolong their grief.

To be sure, there could be alternative explanations for the damaged artifacts, but our identification of these sites as archaeological remnants of camps occupied by Apache laborers is also supported by other archaeological evidence. Cans and buckets punctured by numerous nail holes were identified as probable strainers used in making *tulpai*, a mildly intoxicating beer made from sprouted corn (fig. 4.9). Grills woven from scraps of wire were recognized as holders for roasting ash bread (similar to tortillas) (fig. 4.10), and small *metates* and cobble *manos* (grinding stones) were found.

Other artifacts from the camp sites were less obviously Apache but proved to be distinctive in comparison to non-Apache camps. For example, large buckets and cans, including five-gallon oil and blasting powder cans, were common in the Apache camps. Some had been modified and fitted with wire handles, suggesting that they were reused as storage con-

FIGURE 4.8 The three field photographs show slashed and smashed basins and buckets found at one of the Roosevelt Apache camps. The laboratory photo shows three other pots and pans that have been slashed with an axe or hatchet. These artifacts are interpreted as having been ritually killed when, after their owner died, personal effects were buried or destroyed in conjunction with traditional mortuary ceremonies. (Courtesy of Dames & Moore)

tainers, particularly for water. A few of these large containers found at Apache camps appear to have been ritually killed (fig. 4.11). Other distinctive artifacts commonly associated with the Apache camps were small tin cans with tops partially cut out and then folded back to form handles (fig. 4.12). Such recycling was a general trait of the frontier but was particularly common among the artifact collections from the Apache sites.

Finally, subtly leveled areas ten or twelve feet across, cleared of rocks or in some cases ringed by rocks, were identified as platforms where traditional Apache shelters once stood (fig. 4.13). These wickiups were domes of bent branches covered with brush and often supplemented with canvas and blankets. Nearly 150 suspected wickiup platforms were mapped in five Apache camps in the Roosevelt area. Excavations revealed evidence of hearths in some of the platforms, and in one case, the wickiup appears to have been burned as part of a mortuary ceremony.

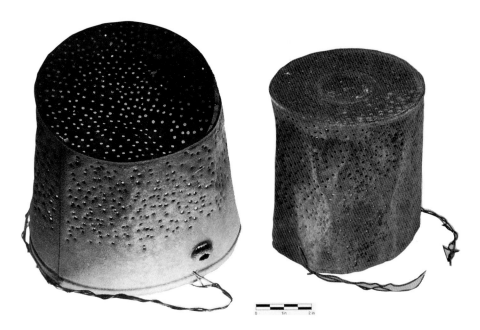

FIGURE 4.9 Apaches punctured cast-off buckets and cans with nails to make strainers used in brewing a mildly intoxicating corn beer, *tulpai*. These tulpai strainers were found at Apache camps at Roosevelt. (Courtesy of Dames & Moore)

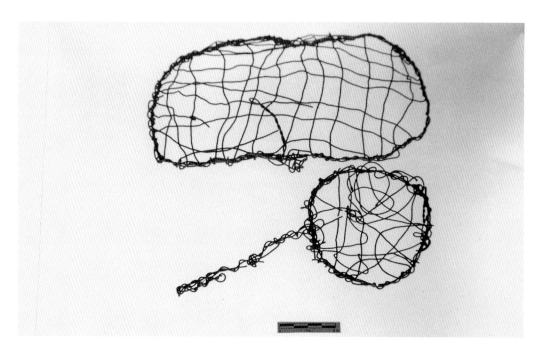

FIGURE 4.10 Apaches wove wire into grills to roast ash bread over an open fire. These ash-bread grills were found by archaeologists at one of the Apache camps at Roosevelt. (Courtesy of Dames & Moore)

These archaeological discoveries were supplemented by oral interviews with Frank Cutter, an Apache who lived in one of the camps when he worked on a maintenance crew along the power canal from about 1918 to 1924 (see "Frank Cutter, Apache Laborer," p. 158). We also discovered a historical novel, *La Paloma*, written by Gustav Harders, a German missionary who lived in Roosevelt during the dam construction era. Despite the obvious bias of a zealous missionary, the novel reveals much about the day-to-day life of the Roosevelt construction camps, especially when read in conjunction with the annual reports Harders sent to his synod board (see "Gustav Harders, Missionary Among the Apaches," p. 162). These disparate lines of evidence, combined with bits of information from other historical documents, offer fresh insight into the Apache experience at Roosevelt.

In total, six Apache camps were found. Detailed study of five of these sites revealed that wickiup platforms were arranged in patterns that probably reflected traditional social relations among nuclear and extended families (fig. 4.14). The largest camp at Roosevelt yielded evidence of wickiups representing almost twenty extended families, indicative of a settlement much larger than traditional camps, perhaps an accommodation to the unusual circumstances at Roosevelt. However, even this large site seems to have been divided into two groups more typical of traditional clusterings.

Historical evidence of the Apaches at Roosevelt includes newspaper accounts of Apache ceremonial "sings" that were attended by non-Apaches and entrepreneurial Mexicans who hawked watermelon and peanuts to the onlookers. The more prominent Apache sings were likely to have been *naihes* ceremonies, which are still held today to commemorate the puberty of young women. The remnants of what appears to be a ceremonial garment were recovered during archaeological excavation of a low, rock-walled windbreak at one of the Apache camps. A cache of more than two hundred colored glass beads, along with even more tinklers (cones made from tin cans), and spangles made from nail plates were found among ashes on the floor of the shelter (fig. 4.15). Buckskin fragments adhering to the artifacts suggest this was probably a naihes dress or poncho (see Ferg 1987 for a color illustration of such a garment), or perhaps a kilt worn by *gaan* (mountain spirit) dancers (also known as crown dancers) during puberty or curing ceremonies. These elaborate garments were generally passed on from generation to generation for reuse, and why one would have been discarded or perhaps burned remains a mystery.

FIGURE 4.11 This bucket, discovered at an Apache camp near Roosevelt, was probably used for carrying and storing water. The slashed bottom indicates it may have been ritually "killed" after the death of its owner. (Courtesy of Dames & Moore)

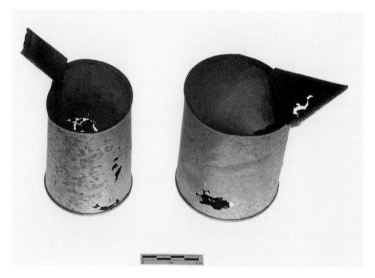

FIGURE 4.12 Cups with handles made by bending back and folding the lids of tin cans were commonly found at the Roosevelt Apache camps. (Similar artifacts have been reported from historic Tohono O'odham saguaro fruit harvesting sites in the southern part of the state [Bruder 1975:288].) (Courtesy of Dames & Moore)

FIGURE 4.13 The only archaeological evidence of most Apache wickiups was a subtle leveling of the ground surface, but occasionally the wickiup locations were outlined with rocks. Nearly 150 wickiup platforms were identified at five Apache camps at Roosevelt. (Courtesy of Dames & Moore)

The artifacts recovered from the Apache camps are typical of other construction camps—mostly tin cans and broken bottles, but the collections are not as varied as those from non-Apache sites, suggesting that although the Apaches had adopted Euro-American manufactured goods, they did so selectively. Although the archaeological remnants are so much like those of non-Apache sites that they are difficult to recognize as Apache, a more-detailed examination revealed that life within the Apache camps at Roosevelt reflected traditional customs to a surprising degree. Aboriginal houses, foods cooked over open fires, traditional social structure, and religious practices all were very much in evidence.

The Apaches at Work

Whether Louis Hill was pleased from the start with his Apache laborers is hard to say. In 1911, when testifying before Congress, he remembered that at first the Apaches had been undernourished and too weak to work hard. He paid them only $1.50 per day until they became stronger, but he quickly came to rate them above Mexican and Anglo workers (Hill 1906; U.S. Congress, House of Representatives 1911). Apache work crews quarried rock, dug canals, helped erect power lines, and worked in the

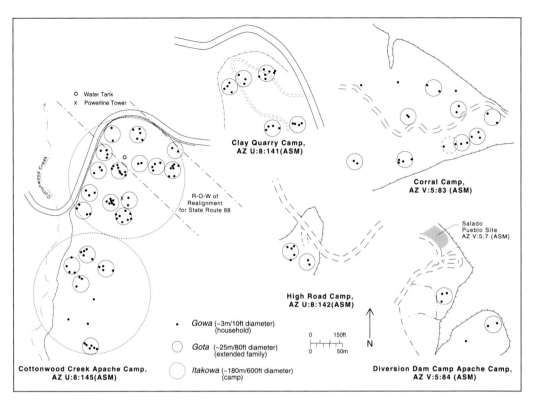

Within the figure the following labels appear:

O Water Tank
X Powerline Tower

Clay Quarry Camp,
AZ U:8:141(ASM)

Corral Camp,
AZ V:5:83 (ASM)

Cottonwood Creek

R-O-W of
Realignment
for State Route 88

Salado
Pueblo Site
AZ V:5:7 (ASM)

High Road Camp,
AZ U:8:142(ASM)

Gowa (~3m/10ft diameter)
(household)

Gota (~25m/80ft diameter)
(extended family)

Itakowa (~180m/600ft diameter)
(camp)

Cottonwood Creek Apache Camp,
AZ U:8:145(ASM)

Diversion Dam Camp Apache Camp,
AZ V:5:84 (ASM)

0   150ft
0   50m
N

FIGURE 4.14 The clustered arrangement of wickiups suggests that individual households (*gowa*) were grouped into extended families (*gota*)—an indication that traditional Apache social structure was intact at the Roosevelt camps. The sizes of the camps varied considerably. At the largest Roosevelt camp, which was much larger than traditional Apache communities, the spatial arrangement suggests that clusters of extended families, in effect, represented two distinct camps (*itakowa*). (Courtesy of Dames & Moore)

cement mill. However, they were valued most for the roads they built, and especially for their skill in dry masonry—laying and fitting rocks without mortar—to construct supports for road embankments through the rugged terrain.

Among their triumphs was the Apache Trail, now part of State Route 88, hewn through the Salt River canyon from Roosevelt to Mesa. The road cost $500,000 and took just over a year to build. It opened in early 1905, and during the first year, 1.5 million pounds of freight passed over the road to the dam site. The second year, tourists began to use the road (Trimble 1986).

A typical Apache work crew consisted of twelve to fourteen men—four to five teamsters and another six to eight men working with shovels. These numbers correspond to the number of men that might have been present in a traditional camp, and it

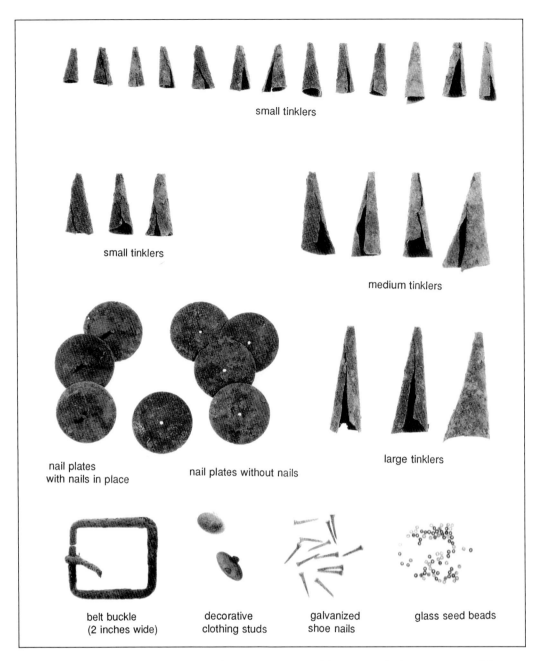

small tinklers

small tinklers

medium tinklers

nail plates
with nails in place

nail plates without nails

large tinklers

belt buckle
(2 inches wide)

decorative
clothing studs

galvanized
shoe nails

glass seed beads

FIGURE 4.15 All of these decorative artifacts were recovered from a single feature at one of the Roosevelt Apache camps and are interpreted as the remains of a ceremonial garment, probably a *naihes* dress worn in a ceremony to celebrate puberty. Why such a valuable garment was discarded is a mystery but its presence suggests that the Apaches continued to practice traditional ceremonies in the Roosevelt camps. (Photograph by Helga Teiwes, Arizona State Museum; courtesy of Dames & Moore)

is reasonable to assume that the social structure of the camps was transferred to the work crews. Some of these crews were supervised by Apache men, most of whom appear to have been traditional clan leaders. These Apache crew bosses earned an average of $80.00 a month, or $3.50 to $4.00 a day, approximately what other subforemen made.

Hill's use of Apache laborers at Roosevelt is generally acknowledged as a key to his success in completing the project. This experience stands in contrast to unsuccessful attempts to employ Indians on other Reclamation Service projects throughout the West. Hill's success was due in large part to his style of labor management, based on his contempt for federal civil service strictures. He and his construction engineer, Chester Smith, resisted attempts of Washington bureaucrats to impose what they viewed as unworkable civil service hiring procedures. Smith (1906:3) specifically stated, "I have no desire to experiment with any gang of shoemakers or pumpkin-rollers such as I would be more than liable to get from a civil service list."

From the Apache perspective, the most important exception to civil service rules was one that allowed several men to share a single job. Provided one man reported for each job each day, supervisors overlooked the Apache approach to wagework. The system worked well, as Reverend Harders observed.

> [The Apache laborer] works perhaps two or three months and then demands four or five months' vacation. So several good friends or relatives club together. One takes a job, and about three families share his income. When he tires of work, another takes his place. In this way they changed off, so that one man's wages support about three families, the income being sufficient for their modest demands.
> With respect to food and living conditions, they are content with the least and simplest. (1968:22)

Perhaps without knowing it, Harders aptly described the gota, or traditional extended family. A man might no longer share hunting duties, but he could share work for wages with his uncles and brothers and divide the income among the extended family. This flexibility allowed the Apaches to adapt their traditions to the world of wagework and sustain the ties and obligations of family and clan so fundamental to their culture.

There is scant evidence that Apache children had any formal schooling at Roosevelt. Reverend Harders' attempt to establish an Indian school lasted less than a year. Instead, Apache children in the camps were raised traditionally.

Early in the Roosevelt Dam project, the San Carlos Indian agent ordered Indian policemen to gather school-age children and any adults who were not usefully employed and return them to the reservation. Many Apaches fled into the mountains to hide. Hill recognized the difficulties he would face if Apache families were broken up, and he wired to Washington to complain. In an unusual move, the San Carlos agent was replaced, and his order rescinded (U.S. Congress, House of Representatives 1911).

Despite the fact that they were part of one of the largest and technologically most complex construction projects in the country, the Apaches at Roosevelt were more free of government bureaucracy and strictures than they were on their reservation. They were certainly more productively employed at Roosevelt than on the reservation, and in a manner that allowed them to maintain many traditional aspects of their culture. Some of the Apaches may also have felt more at home while living in the Tonto Basin because they had been living in the basin, at least seasonally, before the dam construction camps were established (fig. 4.16). As one Apache remembered, "We were happy. We were well fed. We took care of each other like families were meant to" (Cutter 1987).

However, it would be misleading to paint too rosy a picture of the lives of the Apache laborers and their families at Roosevelt. Messianic movements among American Indians were symptomatic of the discontent they felt, and one nativistic movement, called the *Daagodighá* (rising up), was promoted among the Apaches during the Roosevelt construction era.

Followers of Daagodighá believed the earth would be purged of evil (including whites), while believers were raised into the sky. This messianic movement indicates that some of the Apaches were longing for something better than the Roosevelt construction camps (see "The Symbolism of Watering the West," p. 23).

The four decades from 1880 to 1920 have been called the age of assimilation for Native Americans across the United States, their period of most rapid cultural erosion. A superficial history might conclude that because the Apache laborers were almost invisible in the documentary record, they had almost melted into the dominant culture. A more careful analysis of the historical and archaeological record leads to an almost exact opposite conclusion. In the midst of one of the most elaborate engineering projects of the time, the Apaches, paradoxically, seem to have been temporarily sheltered from the bureaucratic attacks of the Office of Indian Affairs and the onrushing twentieth century. For a short time, the Apaches were allowed to live more as Apache than they could have on a reservation.

Other Days, Other Dams

The pace of dam building quickened in central Arizona during the 1920s as four other dams were raised, and it continued into the 1930s and 1940s. Archaeological research at the 1924–1927 construction camp for the Horse Mesa Dam discovered a cluster of destroyed enamelware pots and pans essentially identical to those at Roosevelt, revealing what was very likely an undocumented Apache component of the camp. The archaeological evidence indicates that by the late 1920s, Apache laborers were living in tent houses rather than wickiups and were no longer cooking over open fires.

Snippets of historic documents suggest that some American Indians also worked at Mormon Flat Dam (1923–1926) and at Stewart Mountain Dam (1928–1930), but no archaeological evidence survives to shed more light on those experiences.

FIGURE 4.16 These Apache wickiups were photographed near Roosevelt on June 22, 1899, during an early survey of the Tonto Basin for a reservoir site. Although of poor quality, the photo nevertheless documents the presence of Apaches in the area before dam construction began. The photographer, identified only as "FHN," probably was Frederick H. Newell, who was named chief engineer of the Reclamation Service when it was established three years later. (Courtesy of the National Archives)

Limited oral history evidence indicates a few Indians may have been employed in the 1926–1927 Camp Pleasant on the Agua Fria River. Apparently, about a dozen Indians, probably Yavapais, worked on the 1936–1939 construction of Bartlett Dam.

The role of the Apaches at Roosevelt was never duplicated in the historic dam construction camps of central Arizona. Construction work became more mechanized, and as the national economy crashed into the Great Depression, the labor shortage of the early days of the century disappeared, and then became a surplus. As most of the opportunities in the construction business evaporated, American Indians were again victims of discrimination. During the construction of Bartlett Dam, the site was flooded badly in February 1937 and again in March 1938. James Gibson, secretary and treasurer of the Arizona Lumber Company, which undoubtedly made a tidy profit while supplying lumber for Bartlett Dam, as well as for Mormon Flat, Horse Mesa, and Stewart Mountain dams during the 1920s, noted that

> the flood waters rose so high that they washed about every loose piece of lumber . . . right on down the river. Now there is a large reservation of Indians located below . . . Well, by golly, they got their old horses out and their lasso ropes and hauled those drifting timbers out of that stream and actually built livable houses out of them. So, you see, we are helping build the world's largest multiple arch dam and solving the housing problem of the Indians, both at the same time. (*Arizona Builder and Contractor* 1938)

Although Mr. Gibson reveals some admiration of the Indians' resourcefulness, it is doubtful that he was aware of the crucial role Indian laborers had played in building the mighty Roosevelt Dam some three decades earlier. Native Americans had become only bit players in the dam-building business, reduced to salvaging the dregs.

In the early part of this century, the attitude of construction managers and the press toward wageworkers at Roosevelt—whether Anglo, Mexican, Indian, or Asian—reflected a mixture of antipathy, ambiguity, ambivalence, and astonishment. The use of ethnic labels to categorize laborers was typical throughout the United States and the West at the time.

In 1905, Louis Hill, the supervising engineer for the Roosevelt Dam project, wrote to his superior expressing concerns about the high turnover rate among common laborers. He described the Roosevelt work force as part of a "floating population" who worked just long enough to obtain a "stake," which varied between one day's pay up to $400 or $500, "depending usually on the man and the amount of 'drunk' he thinks he can stand." Some workers used their stakes to start prospecting, but most would "squander" their money "from one to five days after they reach town" (1905).

A year later, Hill wrote another letter (1906) describing the general character of the laborers as

> rather low grade—Indians, Mexicans and whites—their value in about the order written. The nationality of the laborers of various classes, outside of the Indians and Mexicans, are from all parts of the world, Italians, Swedes, Danes, hoboes, besides Americans from nearly every state and territory. The average length of service of a laborer on any job is about ten days, although, of course, there are laborers who have worked for us two years, and others work only two hours. The usual way is for a laborer to work until he has saved his "stake" and then he goes to Mesa or Globe and blows it in.

In the same letter, Hill complained that the "labor material is poor and there is very little of it," and that during the hot summer, the only workers who remained at Roosevelt were those who had good positions or who were "too lazy to walk." In the relatively warm winter, however, workers stayed longer. "It seems to be a good place," Hill concluded, "for the hobo to spend his vacation."

Local newspaper editors often displayed open hostility towards the immigrant laborers at Roosevelt. In 1905, a Globe newspaper editor declared it "impossible to keep enough high grade white labor in camp to make a satisfactory leaven for the mass of Indians, Mexicans and European foreigners who have congregated in the Salt River basin" (ASB 10 Aug 1905). Later that year, the same editor ranted against an unfortunate Mexican worker who had developed epilepsy and become a ward of Gila County as an example of the "misfit, imported peons who bring their diseased bodies, weak intellects and criminal tendencies into the territory to replace a higher grade of labor" (ASB 26 Oct 1905).

It is curious that some of the descriptions of the quality of Indian labor lack the ethnocentric venom aimed at Hispanics. Instead, a mix of surprise, paternalism, and racism colors the comments of observers at Roosevelt. Frederick Newell, chief of the Reclamation Service during the construction of Roosevelt Dam, expressed amazement at the response of such a "blood-thirsty" people. "When paid a white man's wages for a white man's work," he declared, "they have adopted a white man's clothes and have been not only faithful but have proved unusually intelligent in their work" (Newell 1920:35).

Similar positive reactions to specific experiences with ethnic groups of laborers stood as counterexamples to the popular stereotypes (e.g., Steiner 1979), but a dual labor structure proved to be pervasive throughout the West. The bottom-tier, low-paying jobs came to be so dominated by ethnic minorities that even whites who took such work suffered a loss of status (White 1991).

JERRY JONES

Robert "Jerry" Jones, the only African American known to have worked at Camp Dyer, hired on with the Agua Fria Construction Company in January 1893. When Jones arrived at the camp, construction activities had been underway for nearly a year. Initially, he was assigned to one of the twelve-man teams excavating and clearing the foundation for the Dyer Diversion Dam, but he was working at the corral, evidently tending the horses and mules used in the construction work, when a "cloudburst came down the Agua Fria and washed away [the construction] derricks and appliances" (Maricopa County Records 1927b).

The project was abandoned, and all the workers left Camp Dyer except for Jones. He sued for back wages along with the other laborers, apparently not having been paid for almost half a year, but Jones settled up with William Beardsley, who hired him to live at Camp Dyer as a caretaker until Beardsley could arrange for additional financing to complete the construction.

When he took the job, Jones, a bachelor, could not have suspected that he would live at Camp Dyer, apparently alone except for occasional visitors, for the next twenty-one years. One source describes the remnants of Camp Dyer in 1896 as a large "house," two small "houses" covered with tents, a barn, and a corral (Maricopa County Records 1896e). In 1903, an engineering consultant hired by Beardsley took a photograph of Jones at Camp Dyer (Schuyler 1903) (fig. 4.17).

A 1906 map identifies "Jerry's Place" near the diversion dam (Arizona Consolidated Development Company), and Mrs. Bessie Champie Morgan, a longtime resident of Tip Top, a mining town to the north, recalled in an interview that when they traveled to Phoenix, they often stopped overnight at a stage station operated by a Negro (Fireman 1963). Robert Beardsley also stated that his father, William, supplied Jones with some horse feed to sell to travelers, confirming that Jones did convert Camp Dyer into an informal stage stop (Maricopa County Records 1927b).

His caretaker duties for Beardsley involved measuring flows of the Agua Fria River twice daily, but more importantly, his presence on site supported Beardsley's contention that he was diligently pursuing completion of the irrigation project, which helped to preserve his claimed water rights. Beardsley did not pay Jones any wages during the twenty-one years he lived

FIGURE 4.17 Consulting engineer James Schuyler took this photograph at Camp Dyer in 1903 and wrote his own caption: "Robt. Jones, or 'Jerry' as he is generally called, is the faithful old negro watchman who has lived alone in charge of the property for eight years past [since 1895]. He was induced to sit for his portrait with his only companion, a little dog, in his lap. Incidentally, the Lidgerwood cableway, the cement house, tank, and a corner of the boarding house are shown."

at Camp Dyer, but when Jones retired to Phoenix in 1916, Beardsley paid him a lump sum of $1,000 on his "account." Jones, who had probably never seen so much money, was unaccustomed to the urban ways of Phoenix and was a "broken" man within months. Beardsley explained that "the darkies here in town, the gamblers and some of the Mexican women had gotten [the money] away from him and he was in trouble" (Maricopa County Records 1927b).

William Beardsley and, later, his son Robert adopted a paternalistic role, paying Jones $10 a week. Court records document that Jones was alive in 1927 when he testified at a trial. How much longer he lived and whether the Beardsleys ever balanced out the "account" of their faithful servant are unknown.

CHINESE LIQUOR BOTTLES

Despite the ethnic and cultural pluralism of the historic American West, there are few obvious clues regarding ethnicity in the archaeological record. A typical collection of artifacts from any of the investigated dam construction sites includes tins cans, broken glass bottles, pieces of broken ceramic dishes, nails, buttons and buckles, and an assortment of bits of hardware. Such artifacts provide valuable information about what people ate and drank, how they dressed, what medicines they used, and what type of shelters they lived in, but these collections usually offer few clues about their ethnic affiliations because everyone in the West depended on the same, rather tenuous supply lines for goods.

One exception to this general rule is a group of distinctive artifacts commonly associated with the presence of Chinese who prized certain products from their homeland and went to considerable effort and expense to acquire them. The most common of these artifacts are ceramic dishes and liquor and foods such as soy, hoisin and oyster sauces, sesame seed and rapeseed oils, pickled or dried vegetables and fish, bean curd, and shrimp paste, which were imported in shiny, brown-glazed stoneware containers (fig. 4.18). Because the Chinese were held in such low regard by most of the society, these items were seldom used by anyone other than Chinese, so when recovered archaeologically, they are a strong indication of the actual presence of Chinese.

FIGURE 4.18 This Chinese liquor bottle was recovered during excavations at the Phoenix Chinatown (Rogge and others 1992), but fragments of a few similar liquor bottles and ceramic food jars recovered from the Roosevelt historical archaeological sites attest to the presence of a few Chinese in the camps. (Courtesy of Dames & Moore)

Chinese ceramics, including fragments of the distinctive brown-glazed ceramic food containers and liquor bottles and pieces of a Chinese tea bowl, were found at four of the archaeological sites near Roosevelt Dam. The recovery of these ceramics from Government Hill and from a trash pit at the Cement Mill Camp (probably associated with a temporary camp occupied by Reclamation Service employees) are not too difficult to explain. It is known that the Reclamation Service employed a few Chinese as cooks. However, the brown-glazed ceramic fragments also were recovered from the Diversion Dam Apache camp, the High Road Apache camp, and from other contexts at the Cement Mill Camp, which also had evidence of Apache use.

Although it is unlikely that the Chinese and Apache workers lived in the same camps, there is evidence of interaction between them. One newspaper account documents that Apache men rescued one of the Chinese cooks from drowning as he tried to swim across the Salt River after hunting on the north side (AR 4 Mar 1905), and oral history reveals that Chinese farmers hired Apaches to work in their fields. One Chinese farmer is reported to have been fluent in the Apache language (Cutter 1987).

We suspect that interaction between the Chinese and Apaches offered Apaches the opportunity to salvage some of the

Chinese ceramic vessels once they were emptied of their contents. A Chinese liquor bottle would have made an excellent, although fragile, canteen.

The Roosevelt findings do not negate the rule of thumb about the distinctive brown-glazed ceramics indicating the presence of Chinese, but they do provide a cautionary tale regarding how at least one other distinctive cultural group, the Apaches, probably salvaged the emptied containers for reuse until they were broken and discarded at their camps.

DAM BUILDERS: SOME INDIVIDUAL STORIES

Wageworkers, along with other ordinary folks, seldom make it into history books, and the laborers who worked on the dams of central Arizona are no exception. Records simply do not exist to reveal much of their lives as individuals, but their names and a few biographical snippets have been pieced together, primarily from oral histories, many collected by sociologist Phylis Martinelli during research on the Italian community in Globe. This information provides a glimpse of what the dam construction experience meant for a sample of workers, especially for some of the immigrants attracted to Arizona to see what the American West had to offer.

Simon Abel (*nee* Simone Abello), a stonemason from the village of Stroppo in Piedmont, Italy, traveled to Australia, Africa, and South America as a young man. After marrying, Simon and his wife immigrated to Buenos Aires, Argentina, where two sons were born. Simon's brother Frank, who had worked in the 1892–1895 Camp Dyer, convinced him that Arizona offered more promise, so he left his family in 1901 and traveled to Globe, where he went to work in the mines. He filed a declaration of intent to become an American citizen in 1902 and was able to send for his family within two years. Simon's skills as a stonemason were in demand when Roosevelt Dam was under construction, and he worked there for several years. His family lived in Globe during this time, but Simon visited frequently. After completing his stint on the dam, he first opened a shoe repair business in Globe, and later a store, which remained in operation long after his death.

Jack Giachetti also worked as a stonemason at Roosevelt, and like Simon Abel, he was from Italy, born in the town of Sale in Piedmont. While living in Globe, he married a woman he met there who was from his hometown in Italy. She was the youngest sister of John A. B. Caretto, a baker. Jack and his wife eventually achieved their dream of returning to live in their birthplace.

Joe Perlino's sister was the wife of John Caretto, and he lived with them in the "Panama Section" of Globe's Italian community. Joe was a skilled blacksmith who plied his trade during the construction of Roosevelt Dam. Once the dam was completed, Joe moved back to Globe and remained there for the rest of his life.

Enrico Troglia was another stonemason from Piedmont, Italy, who worked on the Roosevelt Dam. He decided to immigrate after being contacted by a *paesani* (labor broker). 'Rico was undoubtedly popular in the Roosevelt camps because he loved to play his concertina, sing, and tell ghost stories. On one of his trips into Globe, 'Rico met Pomposa Guzman, who had also come from Italy, and whom he later married. The marriage was blessed with thirteen children. After Roosevelt Dam was completed, 'Rico went to work in the Old Dominion mine and lived out his life in Globe. He died in 1933 of silicosis, a lung disease undoubtedly caused by a lifetime of breathing mine dust.

Thomas Quarelli was another stonemason from Piedmont, Italy. He first came to Arizona in 1893 to work in the mines at Morenci, but he had moved to Globe by 1897. In 1905, he traveled back to Italy, where he married Clotilde Ricca, but he soon returned to Arizona to work as a mason at Roosevelt, leaving his wife and son in Italy. He had saved enough to send for his family by 1908. In 1911, when Roosevelt Dam was completed, the Quarellis moved to the mining town of Winkleman, where Quarelli went into the mercantile business. He prospered for many years, and almost seven decades later, the community changed the name of Front Street to Quarelli Street to honor the immigrant family.

Frank Pendley, Sr., born in Austin, Texas, in 1877, came to Roosevelt in his mid-twenties to work as a driller quarrying stone. He apparently did not stay long because he worked as a miner in the Mayer-Humboldt area of central Arizona from 1907 to 1910, later moving farther north to homestead along Oak Creek. Where others had not dared to attempt homesteading, Frank succeeded, in part because of skills he practiced in the Roosevelt quarries. In order to bring an irrigation ditch to his fields, he had to excavate two tunnels through sheer sandstone cliffs ninety feet above the creekbed. After two years of effort, the canal was completed, and Frank began a successful career raising apples and other fruits and vegetables.

Frank married in 1921 at the age of forty-four, and he and his wife continued to live on the property until he died in 1954. The farm remained in the family until it was acquired for the Slide Rock State Park. The Pendley Ditch, its tunnels, and some of the surviving historic buildings on the farm were recently listed on the National Register of Historic Places.

Joaquin Imperial, a Mexican American who worked on the construction of Waddell Dam in 1926 and 1927, is one of the few Hispanic laborers known by name. His father had been born in Florence, his mother in Yuma. Joaquin, born in 1909, was one of ten children. The family moved frequently around southern Arizona as his father worked at a variety of jobs— farming, building railroads, operating a grocery and dry goods store in Superior, and prospecting for gold when there was no other work. Later, the senior Imperial operated a store in Chandler until he carried too much credit and went out of business.

When he was about eighteen, Joaquin took his first construction job and helped build Lake Pleasant Dam. He remembered some of the work as being particularly hard, especially unloading one-hundred-pound sacks of cement from railroad cars at Marinette, but he was thankful to have a job that paid thirty-five to forty cents an hour. His parents and two siblings lived in a tent on the west side of the river, an unplanned overflow section of the camp, until his mother's illness forced them to move to Glendale. After that, Joaquin commuted in a Model T Ford with four other laborers, working a total of about a year and a half on the project.

After Imperial completed his stint at the dam, he worked at a variety of jobs around the valley, including fourteen years at the Crystal Ice factory in downtown Glendale. Severe asthma forced him into early retirement. Joaquin was the only laborer to be honored when the sixtieth anniversary of the completion of Waddell Dam was celebrated in 1987.

Stories of individuals are the most effective antidote to stereotypes, and these few glimpses into the lives of dam construction workers clearly indicate that their experience at the dams of central Arizona played remarkably varying roles in their lives. For some immigrants, the construction jobs were the start of new careers in a new land. For others, their time in the construction camps was a temporary job before they returned to their home countries. The dam construction work may have taught them skills they used in later life, and for some, it may have been an episode fondly recalled as a highlight in a long laboring career.

FRANK CUTTER, APACHE LABORER

Anthropologist Betsy Brandt and archaeologist Everett Bassett visited Frank Cutter (fig. 4.19), a Tonto Apache, at his house on the San Carlos Reservation on a chilly morning in February 1987. A barrel-chested man wearing dungarees, a flannel shirt, and work boots, eighty-one-year-old Frank was still a vigorous man with vivid memories. Two months later, a road trip that the three made to Roosevelt awakened additional memories for Frank. An Apache interpreter helped during some of the interviewing, but Frank spoke English at times, always using the present tense even when remembering the old days.

Frank was too young to have worked on the construction of Roosevelt Dam, having been born on February 7, 1906, but his mother's father, John Casey, worked with pick and shovel on one of the Apache road-construction crews. Before coming to work on the dam, Mr. Casey had scouted for the U.S. Army at San Carlos, and he trapped and hunted in the Tonto Basin long before dam construction began. Frank remembered his grandfather John telling him about having to awaken at 3:00 A.M. each morning to run to the work sites along the Apache Trail.

As a boy, Frank grew up at Wheatfields, a settlement on Pinal Creek between Globe and Roosevelt. At the age of eight or nine, he entered the local grade school at the urging of his Mexican stepfather, and he recalled earning school lunch money by working in vegetable fields run by a Chinese family.

Right across there were vegetable fields run by a Chinaman. That's where the Indian people used to work, for a dollar a day, sometime seventy-five, fifty cents a day. That was 1917 and I used to be around in there when I was a boy, when I was a little kid. And I still remember that. Joe—I remember he was named Joe. There was about eight or nine Chinese running that little patch there. Cabbage, potatoes, onions, lettuce, all kind of vegetables. One Chinese was working here, he can speak Apache the same as we do. I don't know where in the world they learn to speak Apache.

FIGURE 4.19 Frank Cutter worked on a maintenance crew approximately a decade after the completion of Roosevelt Dam. He willingly shared his memories and was a valuable source of oral history regarding the Apache experience at Roosevelt. (Courtesy of Diana Hadley)

Frank also remembered a Mexican resident of Wheatfields who spoke Apache. Mr. Cutter's mother, Ann Casey, farmed in the Wheatfields area. "And here, my mother used to live right in there in 1920, and this was a little field we were supposed to take care of. Carrots, turnips, we haul it on a wagon team to Globe-Miami." They sold the produce to miners, but Frank said, "You can't make money. It's only a dime a pack. Everything was cheap at that time. You can get a dime for bread, French bread, and get your shirt for seventy-five cents, and Levi Strauss, dollar and a half."

In the early 1920s, Frank attended the high school in Globe and had a summer job on a crew that maintained the Roosevelt power canal. He was paid $2.50 a day to trap the gophers that burrowed into the power canal, saving the gopher tails to show to his boss. At times, the crew lived at the Corral Camp, one of the archaeological sites we investigated. The work crew moved from the Corral Camp downstream to Grapevine, Porter Spring, and Cottonwood Creek as they cleaned out and repaired other sections of the canal. Other Apaches who worked on the crew from time to time included Frank's brother Ernest,

Sam Yesterday, Jim Lane, Ross and Jim Steel, Fred Casey, Scott Early, and Ed Gilson, whom Frank described as an educated Apache who served as the crew foreman.

In the summer floods of the mid-1920s, the brush diversion dam had to be rebuilt more than once. Frank recalled that the Salt River Valley Water Users' Association routinely hired forty to fifty Apaches for the work, and occasionally as many as fifty Yaqui Indians living in the Salt River Valley were employed as well and lived at the "intake camp." "When the [diversion] dam wash out, the people was brought out from the [San Carlos] reservation by agency. And they begin to work here to help us to build that dam. The dam is all been washed out every time in summertime. They call it 'the place where the dam busts open.' "

Work in the Apache camps was divided along gender lines. Apache men worked as laborers while the women worked in the camps caring for children, preparing food, tanning leather, weaving baskets, and building wickiups. Dam construction work contributed a new element to traditional wickiup construction, canvas bags.

> They have to bring in the limb of a tree and dig a hole right around like planting a tree. Then get the top, bend it down, and tie it with a yucca rope—you have to mash that up and make a string out of it and tie it. And then you go ahead and get the wheat, whatever you run into, and just cover it up with. But mostly the bear grasses—the bear grasses won't leak. When they work, they used to have a canvas cement bag. They used to save them, sew them up together, and make a canvas out of it. And that would go on top of the bear grass. Whenever the job was over, they can move out.

Although Frank remembered the Apaches collecting wild foods such as acorns, yucca fruit, berries, and fish, Apache laborers spent part of their wages to purchase food. Frank described "grocery shopping" while working at Roosevelt in the early 1920s as "a hard way to get the groceries, but anyway, once a week, one of you [non-Indians] use to bring a load of groceries, some slab of bacon, flour, beans, potatoes, sugar, coffee, coming in an old truck from Phoenix. I think that's where they come from."

Apache men took traditional sweat baths about once a week, on Sunday when they did not have to work. The baths served to "keep them strong" as well as cleanse their bodies. Although

Apache women built residential wickiups, Apache men built the special structures for the sweat bath along the Salt River because "you have to dive in the river when you get hot."

While at Roosevelt, Apache people dealt with death in their traditional way. The body was buried under rocks in an isolated cave; no one was buried near the camps. Personal possessions such as blankets and clothing were burned; those that could not be burned were "killed." "If one in the family die, they have to put the fire in that building and chop up all the dishing outfit [pots and pans], make a hole in it so they wouldn't be no use no more after that."

However, over the decades, Mr. Cutter observed the degeneration of some traditional cultural practices.

> One time I remember, they had a little powwow here for these people. They dance for a night because they want to make a sing for someone or another. They sang all night and dance until sunrise and pray. There was no liquor at that time, nobody drunk. That was in the good old day.
>
> Lot of tulpai parties, sometimes, but not all the time like now. At that time, different. They don't have to bother each other. Whoever had the tulpai, he can call his friend, notify his friend to visit. But not other people to go ahead and join in by themselves, the way they do now.

Frank began farming along upper Tonto Creek near Gisela in the mid-1920s but lost the arable land in a flood. He then worked on a rock crusher and sorted ore at a Tonto Basin quicksilver mine on Mt. Ord, a mine that operated from 1925 until 1932. He moved back to San Carlos in 1928 to work on the railroad relocation made necessary by the construction of Coolidge Dam, which inundated part of the reservation. Within a decade, almost all the Apache laborers were forced back to the reservation as construction firms began using more and more heavy equipment. As Frank recalled, "When big equipment came in, the non-Indian took the construction job. Also they began to become a union and these Indian, they don't even realize about union. So all the Tonto moved into the reservation and some have to move back to Payson, in 1935."

Some Apaches continued to live in the Roosevelt area until about 1937, but during the Great Depression, they returned to the San Carlos Reservation hoping to find work at the new Civilian Conservation Corps (CCC) camp. Employment by the CCC led to the abandonment of traditional Apache housing because "when the Three-C [CCC] began to open in reservation we still live in the Apache way. But after all they deduct about ten dollars a month out our wages to save for the agency to buy stove and a tent. When we get enough money deduction, enough to buy a stove and a tent, we get it. We keep it. It's ours. Because we pay for it. From there on, some people began to build a house. And now, they all live in a house."

One of the Apache names for the Roosevelt area translates as "rock house packed together," an obvious reference to the cliff dwellings now designated as the Tonto National Monument. Frank and his contemporaries were clearly aware of the many prehistoric archaeological sites in the area. "At that time, we respect that kind of outfit, the old ruin. They are old people, about a thousand years ago. We don't bother that kind. As long as we live here, we just leave it alone."

In many ways, Frank Cutter's way of life in the 1910s, 1920s, and 1930s seemed almost as remote as that of the "old people" of the prehistoric past. While driving to Roosevelt, Frank saw that his old grade school at Wheatfields had been demolished, and "no trespassing" signs blocked the access to his old home. It is easy to understand why he is nostalgic about the "good old days" at Roosevelt.

GUSTAV HARDERS, MISSIONARY AMONG THE APACHES

Gustav Harders (fig. 4.20), born in Germany in the mid-1860s, immigrated to the United States at the age of twenty-four. He completed his theological studies and served as a popular and respected pastor of the large Jerusalem Lutheran Church in Milwaukee for eighteen years. An illness, probably tuberculosis, forced Harders to make a drastic career change at the age of 42. He moved to the Arizona Territory to work as a missionary among the Apaches, arriving in the Roosevelt construction camps in 1907.

Harders was a slightly built man, described as a poet and eccentric. Despite his frail health, his annual reports to his synod board demonstrate that he labored assiduously to convert the Apaches to Christianity, struggling to learn the difficult Apache language so that he could preach to them in their native tongue. He never mastered English very well, but he managed to communicate sufficiently to give religious instruction to a group of Chinese laborers in Globe as well (Sauer, Johne, and Wendland 1992). He died a decade after arriving in Arizona.

FIGURE 4.20 Missionary Gustav Harders spent nearly a decade among the Apaches of Arizona. His experiences were the basis for three popular historical novels that he published in his native Germany. (Courtesy of Northwestern Publishing House)

During his years in Arizona, Harders apparently led an ascetic life, often arising at 5:00 A.M. to write. He produced three novels that were published in German by the Rauhe Haus of Hamburg. One was a best-seller in Germany, and all were widely read there and in the United States. They were subsequently translated and published in English:

1953 *Yaalahn* (originally published in German as *Jaalahn*). Henry C. Nitz, translator. Northwestern Publishing House, Milwaukee.

1958 *Dohaschtida* (originally published in German as *Wille Wider Wille*). Alma Pingel Nitz, translator. Northwestern Publishing House, Milwaukee.

1968 *La Paloma.* Henry C. Nitz, translator. Northwestern Publishing House, Milwaukee.

La Paloma, named after a Mexican song Harders came to love, is a thinly veiled autobiographical novel set in the Roosevelt construction camps. Although not many whites would have befriended Hispanics in those times, the story describes a warm friendship that developed between the protagonist, a missionary, and a Hispanic fellow who operated a restaurant in the town of Roosevelt. In one scene, a blind Hispanic street musician plays the song "La Paloma" while the missionary eats in a Chinese restaurant in Globe, a reflection of the ethnic mixture of the community.

Other interesting details that emerge in the novel are the shrill whistle that signaled the end of the work day, people's fear of crossing the suspension bridge swaying high above the Salt River (the only connection with O'Rourke's Camp), and the community's sorrow over a young woman dying as she gave birth to twins.

Some of the most interesting aspects of the novel, especially when read in conjunction with a separate paper that Harders published, *Die Heutigen Apachen* (The Modern Apaches), are the descriptions of the Apache camps.

> Even today the Apaches do not live in houses. The women build the huts in which they live and which they greatly prefer over houses. These dome-shaped brush huts are built with canvas, if they can raise the money. If not, they use flour sacks, or even the poorer ones use old clothes or potato sacks. There is not much to say about the furniture inside. In the middle, a fire burns continuously on the ground. In a circle around the fire, blankets are thrown on the ground on which they sleep at night or lay about on during the day. Besides the blankets, one can see a sack of flour, a coffee grinder, tin cans of coffee, sugar, fat, baking powder, salt, and various cooking and eating utensils. Now and again one finds a trunk, sewing machine, lantern, or a couple of small boxes. (translated, 1912:16)

Harders also describes the typical Apache diet, which consisted

> almost exclusively of very strong, sweet coffee, much meat, and very heavy glutinous bread that is made fresh for every meal, but it is not really baked. Water, flour, and baking powder are kneaded into a sticky dough. Small pieces of dough are flattened into a large pancake and it is baked over an open fire or heated or roasted over a warm piece of sheet metal. It takes very few minutes. Often the bread is not really cooked. Only an Indian stomach can tolerate eating and digesting it. (translated, 1912:16–17)

Harders also recognized and recorded the despair of the Apaches, including one young man from the reservation who had just learned to drink whiskey. "He reported it was painful for him, but he is good at it now, and proud of it! Yes, they all drink, like to drink, and feel they must drink in order to tolerate their misery. Because of their circumstances, mothers feel they must teach their children to drink so that they can tolerate their lives" (translated, 1912:17).

One incident described in *La Paloma* is the protagonist's treatment of an elderly Apache woman whose foot had become badly infected.

> They found the aunt in an uncongenial mood. She had not slept all night. She was sitting on the ground, her scraggly dog on her lap. Her badly swollen foot was near the campfire. She had covered the foot with hot ashes, hoping the heat would relieve the pain. Her tousled, unkempt hair, turning gray, hung dishevelled about her head. . . . When he had washed the dirt from the foot, the missionary found a considerable amount of pus which would have to be removed. Without hesitation, and without even asking the woman for her permission, he took a knife from his pocket and made a deep incision into the sore spot. When she felt the sudden pain, she cried out and struck the missionary on the side of his head with all her might. He was not a little frightened at this unexpected gesture of "gratitude." But instead of getting angry or being offended, he slowly turned about, pointed to his other cheek, and said, "Nkoh alchdo!" That is, "Strike me here also." (1968:121–122)

This incident undoubtedly reflected Harder's own struggle to do what he thought was best for the Apaches, although they often did not appreciate his efforts. He clearly was sympathetic to the plight of the Apaches and less biased than many other whites, yet he was clearly ethnocentric in many aspects of his dealings with the Apaches. There is a hint that perhaps Harders understood more than he cared to admit; in *Dohaschtida*, one of his Apache characters, muttering through clenched teeth to the missionary (a fictionalized Harders), says, "I know what you want. You want to rob us. All you palefaces have ever wanted since you came to our country was to take from us. And you are the worst. You want to take the last remaining pleasure, the only thing that makes life worth living. . . . You want us to stop hating, which is our only motive for living" (1958:4–5).

5

Continuity and Lessons

This bottom-up history of the temporary dam construction camps of central Arizona is a story about the lives of ordinary people. We have shifted the focus away from the mythical images of cowboys and Indians, and beyond the battles of power brokers over financing and water policy. By considering the "cowboys of construction" and the reality of wagework, we have offered a broader perspective on the participants and processes of development of the American West.

It would be easy to think of the historic dam construction camps of central Arizona as small, temporary, out-of-the-way communities that provide interesting vignettes of local history, but which are largely irrelevant and trivial aspects of the state's history. We suggest, instead, that these camps are microcosms that reveal patterns and trends characteristic of much of Arizona.

First, the camps were not particularly small in comparison to other settlements (compare figs. 5.1 and 5.2). In 1900, Tucson, the largest city in the territory, had only 7,531 residents, and Phoenix only 5,544. With a population of more than 2,000 residents, Roosevelt, although not formally recognized as such, was among the ten largest communities in the Arizona Territory (Sargent 1988). The other dam construction camps ranged from approximately a hundred to several hundred residents, which would have made them comparable to many contemporary communities.

. . . by dissolving the great divide between the "Old West" and the "New West," [the New Western History] simply does a better job of explaining how we got to where we are today.

—PATRICIA NELSON
LIMERICK (1991:87)

FIGURE 5.1 (overleaf) Tent houses were the dominant form of architecture in the new town of Roosevelt, built uphill and about one-half mile east of the original Roosevelt town site, which was flooded in late 1908. Note the Apache wickiups in the background. (Photograph by Walter Lubken, courtesy of the National Archives)

Admittedly, the camps were temporary, but this also was characteristic of many places in Arizona. A simple experiment, counting one hundred named settlements listed in an Arizona place names book (Granger 1983), revealed that two-thirds of these communities had disappeared since their founding. Perhaps the certainty of the temporariness of the construction camps from the day they were established was atypical, but transience in settlement characterizes much of Arizona's boom and bust historic development.

Second, the dam construction camps were indeed remote, but they were closely connected to urban settlements and to national and international manufacturing centers. One extreme example demonstrates how these construction camps were linked to the rapidly expanding global network. Archaeological study at the 1924–1927 camp at Horse Mesa recovered meat cans with markings indicating they had been packed in Uruguay. After being shipped thousands of miles to Arizona, the canned meat probably was consumed by Apache wageworkers whose grandfathers had considered beef something to be acquired by raiding local ranches.

An economic connection to the wider world is also displayed in both the origins and multicultural makeup of the work forces at many of the dams. This diversity is especially clear at Roosevelt, where it is well documented that workers of European, African, Asian, and American Indian ethnic backgrounds came together to create a laboring community. Anglo workers from throughout North America and Europe, Mexicans, Mexican Americans, African Americans, Asians, and Apaches all came together in the Roosevelt camps to create a microcosm of Arizona's historical and contemporary populations.

Third, the construction camp populations also reflected the social structure of the larger society. The physical layout of the camps, ethnic divisions in the work force, stereotypical attitudes about different ethnic and racial groups, and the relationship between workers and managers all displayed unmistakable and characteristic features of social-status arrangements in the nation at the time (see "Tent Houses and Social Status," p. 178). Although our understanding of what the wageworkers thought about their own status and roles at the dam is incomplete, the archaeological and historical records document that a multicultural population worked cooperatively, although not without occasional conflict, to construct one of the essential building blocks of modern Arizona—the system of dams that still provides flood protection and a crucial water supply.

From a national perspective, Arizona is still a rather small, remote state with a highly transient population. The history of the temporary dam construction camps of central Arizona parallels some key aspects of our modern lives, perhaps more than we care to admit.

Lessons Learned

History is a moralistic enterprise. Many historians search for the lessons to be learned in their reconstructions of the past, believing that the ultimate purpose of the discipline is to help us recognize the mistakes of the past so they can be avoided as we live our present and future lives.

Although historians may be inclined to seek the "moral of the story," archaeologists are typically more reticent to judge the moral implications of their research. In fact, they have been accused of being amoral (Grimes 1986). The reluctance of archaeologists to champion any particular moral perspective is perhaps due to their broad, cross-cultural approach to human endeavors, which often brings them face-to-face with biased ethnocentrism. They fear committing similar sins.

At the risk of heresy, we close this chapter with some observations on lessons learned from our historical archaeological research at the temporary dam construction camps of central Arizona. We have adopted and adapted the insights and alliterative labels of Patricia Limerick in organizing this discussion (1987, 1990, 1991).

Conquest: A Dominant Theme

The first Spaniards who entered what is now the American West proudly wore the name *conquistadores*, undoubtedly repeating a pattern of conflict witnessed throughout the long course of prehistoric human occupation of the region. Later American settlers found the conqueror label an uncomfortable one. They much preferred to view their hegemony as a new occupation of an empty land. However, new historians of the West, such as Patricia Limerick (1987), have bluntly demonstrated that the land was not empty; wars, declared and undeclared, were waged; and native societies were conquered. The dominant culture in this country is dominant because it conquered those who stood in their way. They won the war.

Euro-Americans, at least until quite recently, were much less uncomfortable with being labeled conquerors of nature. The

The aim of history, then, is to know the elements of the present by understanding what came into the present from the past. . . . The goal of the antiquarian is the dead past; the goal of the historian is the living present.

—FREDERICK JACKSON
TURNER (1891; reprint
1986:254)

The merit of archeology is that it can . . . produce for the aficionado objects of great beauty and grace; it can reveal the history of a people and of mankind; it can contribute toward an understanding of the present; and it may one day be used to test scientifically stated hypotheses about human behavior in general.

—FRANK HOLE and
ROBERT F. HEIZER
(1973:10)

FIGURE 5.2 In 1900, the mining town of Globe was among the five largest communities in the Arizona Territory (Bigando 1989). Although somewhat larger and more permanent, Globe was not much different than the Roosevelt camps shown above. (Courtesy of Robert Bigando)

unsettled wilderness was commonly portrayed as dangerous, an enemy to be subdued and controlled. The movement to reclaim the arid West and make the deserts bloom was based on conquering the rivers of the region and controlling their wildly fluctuating flows. Historian Donald Worster noted that Hoover Dam, the greatest of the region's dams, "has the capacity to stir admiration and renew people's faith in the conquest of nature" (1992:64). However, Worster goes on to argue that human domination of nature is illusory when viewed from the long-term temporal perspective, which is the perspective of archaeologists.

It is a wry paradox that the recently conquered Apaches were used to conquer the Salt River. There is no hint that any of the dam construction camp residents pondered the implications of this philosophy of conquest, or their roles in the battle. The laborers certainly faced danger, perhaps as often as the soldiers and warriors who fought in the wars that conquered the native peoples. Many workers also gave their lives while working in places like Roosevelt, lending a certain legitimacy to the imagery of conquest.

Continuity From Prehistoric to Modern Times

Some historians worry that history seems irrelevant in this era of rapid change (e.g., Hamerow 1985). Such claims of irrelevancy may seem extreme, but common notions of the "frontier" as something that characterized the West of a century or more ago also tend to trivialize the region's history by implying that there is a wide gulf between the past and our modern lives. However, we conclude that the experiences of those who preceded us on this landscape have direct relevance for our lives because we are still struggling with many of the same problems they faced.

The prehistoric Hohokam culture of the Sonoran Desert developed, adopted, and adapted subsistence strategies based on irrigation agriculture. Their farming economy was not unlike that of the early American settlers. To be sure, the Hohokam did not work metal, they did not manufacture machinery, they had no written language, and their world of interactions was much more restricted than that of the Americans of the late 1800s, but they did develop elaborate social and cultural systems and manufacture beautiful crafts. The sophistication of their irrigation systems was not significantly exceeded by the American settlers until dams such as Roosevelt were built.

It should give us pause to know that the prehistoric societies collapsed just about a century before the first Spanish explorers entered the region. Archaeologists have yet to fully reconstruct what happened, but it appears some crucial threshold was crossed. Populations declined, broad expanses of fields were no longer cultivated, and towns with community architecture were abandoned.

This societal collapse may not have been due to some unique event or catastrophe. The triggering factor may have been something that happened many times before, but was like a domino falling and toppling only a few others immediately next to it (Bak and Chen 1991; Lipe 1992). As the society became more complex, and the dominoes more densely packed, the next domino to fall may have toppled most of the others. We commonly think our way of life is more sophisticated than that of ancient prehistoric peoples, but is this just a way of comforting ourselves? Is it possible that our dominoes are even more tightly arranged than those of the prehistoric cultures?

Although the workers who lived in the temporary dam construction camps of central Arizona seem much less remote than prehistoric societies, it is easy to dismiss their history as an inconsequential story of small, insignificant, temporary communities. However, the temporary camps were pockets of urban Arizona comparable to many others, and their transience still characterizes much of the West. It is commonly reported that for every four people who move to Arizona, three move away.

Russell Martin (1992:xv) has argued that Westerners "haven't gotten very good at building towns—true communities." The historic dam construction camps demonstrate that a variety of people could come together in communities, even if temporary, to successfully accomplish a common task. Those communities completed their work and disappeared, but they left a dam system that still plays a critical role in our highly transient communities.

Complexity: Not a Simple Story

There has been a tendency to think of Western history as rather a simple story. In part, this stems from the frontier model propounded by Frederick Jackson Turner (1985) shortly before the turn of the century. His was a broad, powerfully synthetic vision of American settlers moving west into empty territory and being transformed by the experience. Turner argued that the pioneers, having escaped the social and political institutions of the Old World, were freed to govern themselves and pursue the abundant opportunities for individual achievement in the West. This wilderness experience, Turner posited, was the reason democracy flourished in America.

New historians of the West characterize this model as an oversimplified reflection of the perspective of powerful white men in the East. They suggest the story of the West is considerably more complex, and as our research demonstrates, the lives of Western dam construction workers were complex indeed.

It is impressive to recognize how much the relatively small numbers of workers in the temporary construction camps were able to accomplish. Dam construction work forces numbering from a hundred to no more than a couple of thousand were probably not much larger than the work gangs the prehistoric Hohokam mustered to build and maintain their canal systems. The fact that historic workers were able to use animal power and, through time, more and more mechanical power is a significant development in itself, but the more substantial increase in complexity from the prehistoric irrigators to the historic dam construction workers lies in the systems that allowed one generation to pay for massive construction by borrowing against future generations. This required concentrating national resources and power to achieve a common goal.

Historians and archaeologists have long recognized the correlation between the organizational demands of building and operating irrigation systems, the urbanization of populations, the increase of social complexity, and the concentration of political power and wealth in an elite controlling class (Adams 1962; Wittfogel 1957). Worster (1985) has argued that the development of the Reclamation Service and powerful agricultural organizations fits this model of "hydraulic societies."

Wageworkers living in the temporary dam construction camps of central Arizona certainly experienced some of the complexities of the social and economic hierarchies typical of hydraulic societies. The camps were segregated into "haves" and "have-nots," often along racial and ethnic lines. For example, senior employees, who were mostly Anglo males, lived in more substantial and better equipped housing. Although there is little evidence of discrimination in terms of unequal pay for equal work, there does seem to have been discrimination in the form of unequal access to the better-paying jobs. Certainly, the dominant Anglo culture controlled decision making.

Still, the isolation and harsh physical circumstances of the dam construction camps were leveling factors. All of the camp residents were subject to the heat and remoteness. The effect of income differentials was no doubt dampened by the limited range of daily sundries, food supplies, and other consumer goods available in the camps. As seen in the historical and archaeological records, the difference in the standards of living between the top and bottom of the construction camp hierarchy was much narrower than in our modern society.

Converging in the American West

One of the more complex characteristics of the history of the West is how peoples of many different ethnic and cultural groups converged in the region. Limerick (1990) has argued that the concept of a rendezvous provides a more appropriate model of settlement than Turner's model of a frontier steadily moving westward from the East.

Rendezvous, a French word, referred to the annual get-togethers of fur traders, or so-called mountain men, and merchants, who met during the early 1800s in the Rocky Mountains to trade pelts for supplies. The ethnic and linguistic diversity of such meetings was amazing. Participants included French Canadians, Mexicans, Irishmen, Scots, Germans, white Americans, and many distinct American Indian groups. Although these people came together for mutual benefit, the rendezvous was often a tense encounter in which people with little common history competed with one another. The meeting sometimes turned violent.

The dam construction camps of central Arizona, particularly Roosevelt, were rendezvous of sorts and classic examples of what might be the most important aspect of Western history— the formation of a new society by ethnic groups from all over the globe. When cultures collide in such a setting, there may be many outcomes (see "Acculturation," p. 181).

The struggle to capitalize on ethnic diversity is a challenge that confronts Arizona today. Some historians suggest that the "melting pot" model made America great (e.g., Schlesinger 1991). They are convinced that the blending and homogenization of ethnicities is a basic ingredient for democracy—and a necessary foundation for national unity. They see the current trend to celebrate ethnic diversity and cultural pluralism as a threat to the very fabric of American life.

Such perspectives are grounded in the tendency inherent in every ethnic group to ethnocentrism; that is, the propensity of each group to think of its way as the right and only way to live. Others see ethnic diversity as a source of pride and adaptive strength. To them, diversity of culture is a palette of perspectives that can be used to paint new pictures of the future.

Our modern challenge is to prevent ethnic boundaries from becoming "tear here" perforations that rend our society apart, and to celebrate ethnic heritage as a resource enhancing our lives. The Roosevelt Dam construction community stands as an example of many ethnic groups working together to accomplish a job. Later construction camps seem to have been much less ethnically diverse. Some uniformity may reflect the melting pot syndrome—that is, people of various nationalities giving up their ethnicities in their bid to become *Americans*. Also, beginning in the early 1920s, new laws limited both the number and nationality of immigrants, particularly those from southern and eastern Europe, although Mexican immigration increased in the 1920s (Cardoso 1980).

At least some of the decreasing diversity, however, was due to the closing of opportunities. This seems to be most clear in the case of Apache laborers. They were called on to meet a critical labor shortage at Roosevelt, and they met the challenge, but when the labor shortage eased, the Apaches were eased out of their jobs.

The image of Roosevelt Dam is prominently displayed on the Arizona state seal because it is a symbol of the importance that reclaiming the desert has played in the history of the state. We hope readers of this book will come to see the image of Roosevelt Dam not only as a monument to conquering nature, but also as a reminder of how an ethnically diverse community came together in a temporary construction camp to accomplish a job under trying conditions—a symbol of how we can conquer the divisive forces within our own transient communities on the very same landscape.

The term "tent house" may seem like an oxymoron, but these hybrids of wood and canvas were a common type of shelter for decades in Arizona. Their history of development and the variability of their styles are not well documented, but the basic advancement over a simple tent was an internal wooden frame over which canvas was tightly stretched.

Tent houses were common not only in the historic dam construction camps of central Arizona, but also at construction sites in other parts of the West (e.g., Costello and Marvin 1992). They were routinely present in mining communities in Arizona (e.g., Teague 1980), and a postcard of historic Globe indicates that many of the residences of that established mining town were tent houses. They were also popular accommodations in the "lunger" colonies that sprang up for tuberculosis patients in the warm Southwest.

At first glance, the crudeness of tent housing might seem like the ultimate leveler of construction camp residents, but social status is not difficult to display when it is important. Tent houses varied considerably in their appointments and details (figs. 5.3, 5.4, and 5.5).

Many tent houses had wooden floors. One resident of the 1936–1939 Bartlett Dam construction camp remembered that the floor of her tent house had been covered with linoleum (Price and Price 1987). Some had simple canvas roofs, and others had a second, or "fly," roof, apparently to enhance their ability to shed water and, probably more importantly, to keep them cooler during the hot summers. Some were equipped with wooden roofs. Walls of tent houses were often partially framed and commonly equipped with hinged doors. The archaeological recovery of screen springs and broken pane glass indicates that some tent houses in the construction camps also had windows. In steep, rugged terrain, tent houses were often erected on hill slopes by building heavy timber cribbing to create a level floor.

At Roosevelt, social status was also reflected in the topographic location of tent houses. The somewhat more disheveled tent houses on the outskirts of Roosevelt, along the low terrace of the Salt River, were the homes of the lowest-status minorities in the construction community. A more elaborately planned community of tent houses was erected on a higher hill slope for the workers based in O'Rourke's Camp. The Reclamation

FIGURE 5.3 (opposite top) These Government Hill tent houses for bachelor engineers (in an area known as "the Bullpen") were well built and quite precisely aligned, almost in defiance of the steep hillslope. (January 26, 1906, courtesy of the Salt River Project)

FIGURE 5.4 (opposite bottom) Both old and new Roosevelt contained great numbers of tent houses. The wash was hanging out to dry when Walter Lubken took this photograph of Newtown on January 20, 1909, shortly after the town was relocated. (Courtesy of the National Archives)

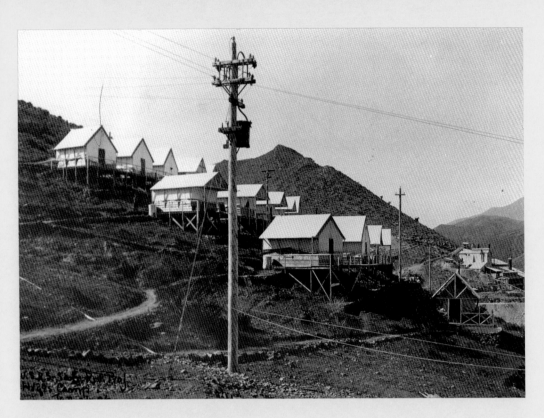

FIGURE 5.5 Inexpensive, cool, and quickly built, the tent house was a common type of residence throughout Arizona. Tent houses often sheltered "lungers" in the tubercular camps of central Arizona, such as the one shown here of Dr. Duffield's office at a sanitarium near Phoenix. The other photograph depicts a man identified only as "Uncle Bob" posing in front of a tent house at the Gilliland Ranch near Oracle, circa 1914. (Courtesy of the Arizona Historical Foundation)

RAISING ARIZONA'S DAMS

Service headquarters, where the elite of the construction community were housed, was on a high finger ridge overlooking both of the lower camps. It was equipped with precisely laid out rows of elaborate tent houses and frame cottages for the senior employees and their families.

ACCULTURATION

Anthropologists have long studied the interactions between cultures when they come in contact, labeling the changes that occur as *acculturation* (e.g., Redfield, Linton, and Herskovitz 1936). Much of the anthropological research of acculturation was undertaken in a colonial context and often focused on changes imposed by imperialistic groups on indigenous ethnic groups. More recent sociological modeling has proposed four outcomes of such cultural encounters: (1) *assimilation*, (2) *integration*, (3) *rejection*, and (4) *deculturation* (Berry 1980).

Assimilation is defined as the loss of identity by one of the interacting cultures and its full engulfment by the dominant culture. Despite the imagery of blending conveyed by the "melting pot" model, much of the incorporation of ethnic groups into American society has, in fact, been assimilation into the dominant Anglo culture.

Integration involves accommodations by both cultures, but maintenance of aspects of both. At the level of individuals, integration could be evidenced by biculturalism or bilingualism. This outcome is akin to the goals of those who promote ethnic or cultural pluralism.

Rejection characterizes the decision of one culture to remain separate from the larger society. Within the context of the study of the dam construction camps, the role of the Apache laborers at Roosevelt might be construed as heading toward integration, but subsequent experiences can be classified as Apache rejection of much of the larger society.

Deculturation is the loss of identity with either of the interacting cultures and leads to a dysfunctional state of cultural marginality. The Apaches who chose to follow millennial movements or who turned to alcohol to forget their lives can be viewed as victims of deculturation.

This classification of acculturation processes is largely descriptive and, as such, may be useful in classifying ethnic group interactions along a continuum of outcomes. However, it does little to explain the processes involved. One reviewer recently concluded that "efforts to depict and measure acculturation as a process have not yet materialized" (Castro 1992:50).

Decades ago, much of the discussion of cultural differences was actually framed in terms of biological variability or race. Earlier generations of anthropologists devoted considerable energy to precise definitions of racial group boundaries, but they soon recognized that race, language, and culture are independent variables. Subsequent demonstration of the essentially continuous nature of biological variation revealed the folly of trying to define pure races. "There is no line across the middle of the Sahara, or the Mediterranean, that divides people into 'white' and 'black,' nor is there a north-south line in Eurasia dividing 'whites' from 'Mongoloids' (or 'Asians')" (Brooks, Jackson, and Grinker 1993:11).

This understanding led to the substitution of the term "ethnicity" for race in trying to understand cultural variability and interaction. Some researchers have adopted a "primordialist" perspective on ethnicity, arguing that the definition of ethnic groups is a natural result of biological characteristics and language. But, clearly, genes are commonly exchanged across ethnic boundaries. Because of the continuous nature of human biological variation, many individuals can make choices in identifying their ethnicity.

At the other end of the spectrum, opposite the primordialists, are the researchers of "instrumentalist" persuasion, who argue that people arbitrarily define their ethnicity based on political and economic goals. They suggest that competing groups will often focus on ethnicity to define boundaries between "haves" and "have-nots" (e.g., McGuire 1982). The promotion of America as a "melting pot" is based on the reverse argument, that elimination of ethnic boundaries will allow all groups equal access to life, liberty, and the pursuit of happiness. However, a simple statement of such creeds does not guarantee economic, political, and social equality, and the shedding of cultural heritage can lead to a state of cultural anomie, or instability.

A basic question to address in searching for a more complete understanding of acculturation processes is, "What factors contribute to the maintenance or elimination of ethnic boundaries in situations of contact between different cultures?" We suspect many factors influence the maintenance or dissolution of ethnic definitions, and that these factors may vary from situation to situation. Although we have yet to satisfactorily explain ethnicity, the concept clearly has significant cultural and historical components, and therefore ethnic group boundaries can be defined and redefined to achieve societal goals. Any label, however, is likely to create stereotypes because it masks recognition and understanding of individuals within labeled groups.

Understanding how ethnic boundaries can be used, or abused, is important for modern America in our continuing struggle to build a healthy, productive society incorporating immigrants from around the globe. Recently, the trend toward global cultural homogenization seems to have been stalled by an increasing number of violent conflicts among ethnic groups. Although such clashes may seem minor when compared to a long-feared global war between superpowers, the ominous pursuit of "ethnic cleansing" is a grim reminder that ethnocentrism remains a powerful force among human societies. The myth of the historic American West as portrayed in Hollywood movies may seem dated and arcane, but as we struggle toward ethnic harmony, a more accurate understanding of the region's multicultural history has broad relevance well beyond the American West.

For Further Reading

This volume represents the first attempt to publish the story of dam construction workers in central Arizona, but much has been written and produced about water and irrigation. A first stop might be the new Arizona Historical Society Museum/ Marley Center in Tempe. Original blocks of stone from the parapet of Roosevelt Dam, removed when the height of the dam was raised, are used to re-create a symbolic dam in the outdoor gallery at the new museum, and interior displays focus on dam construction and the growth of agriculture in the Phoenix area. Exhibits are scheduled to open in the fall of 1995. Other area museums that demonstrate the significance of water in the desert include the Tempe Historical Museum and the History Museum at the headquarters of the Salt River Project in Phoenix.

Several publications provide a broad perspective on water resource development in the American West, or discussions of the general history of the American West from the perspective of the "new" Western history.

Hundley, Norris
   1967   *Dividing the Waters.* University of California Press, Los Angeles.
   1975   *Water and the West: The Colorado River Compact.* University of California Press, Los Angeles.
James, George Wharton
   1917   *Reclaiming the Arid West: The Story of the United States Reclamation Service.* Dodd, Mead, and Co., New York.

Limerick, Patricia Nelson
    1987   *The Legacy of Conquest: The Unbroken Past of the American West*. W. W. Norton & Company, New York.
Limerick, Patricia Nelson, Clyde A. Milner II, and Charles E. Rankin (editors)
    1991   *Trails Toward a New Western History*. University Press of Kansas, Lawrence.
Nash, Gerald D.
    1977   *The American West in the Twentieth Century*. University of New Mexico Press, Albuquerque.
Reisner, Marc
    1986   *Cadillac Desert: The American West and Its Disappearing Water*. Viking Press, New York.
Stegner, Wallace
    1954   *Beyond the Hundredth Meridian: John Wesley Powell and the Second Opening of the West*. Houghton Mifflin, Boston.
Worster, Donald
    1985   *Rivers of Empire: Water, Aridity and the Growth of the American West*. Pantheon, New York.

Charles Sargent succinctly describes the growth of central Arizona and provides a historical context for the temporary dam construction camps. Smith and Zarbin detail the history of the construction of Roosevelt Dam.

Sargent, Charles (editor)
    1988   *Metro Arizona*. Biffington Books, Scottsdale, Arizona.
Smith, Karen L.
    1986   *The Magnificent Experiment: Building the Salt River Reclamation Project, 1890–1917*. University of Arizona Press, Tucson.
Zarbin, Earl
    1984   *Roosevelt Dam: A History to 1911*. Salt River Project, Phoenix, Arizona.

Readers interested in more information about the anthropology of the Western Apache can consult several references.

Basso, Keith H.
    1970   *The Cibicue Apache*. Holt, Rinehart and Winston, New York.
    1971   *Western Apache Raiding and Warfare: From the Notes of Grenville Goodwin*. University of Arizona Press, Tucson.
    1983   Western Apache. In *Handbook of North American Indians*, Vol. 10, *Southwest*, edited by Alfonso Ortiz, pp. 462–488. Smithsonian Institution, Washington, D.C.

Ferg, Alan (editor)

1987   *Western Apache Material Culture.* University of Arizona Press, Tucson.

Opler, Morris E.

1973   *Grenville Goodwin Among the Western Apache.* University of Arizona Press, Tucson.

Several histories focusing on the design and engineering of the dams of central Arizona have been prepared for the Historic American Engineering Record archives.

Introcaso, David M.

1984   *The Roosevelt Power Canal and Diversion Dam.* Historic American Engineering Record No. AZ-4, Salt River Project, Phoenix, Arizona.

1988   *Waddell Dam.* Historic American Engineering Record No. AZ-11, Salt River Project, Phoenix, Arizona.

1989   *Mormon Flat Dam.* Historic American Engineering Record No. AZ-14, Salt River Project, Phoenix, Arizona.

1990   *Bartlett Dam.* Historic American Engineering Record No. AZ-25, Salt River Project, Phoenix, Arizona.

Jackson, Donald, and Clayton B. Fraser

1991   *Horseshoe Dam.* Historic American Engineering Record No. AZ-24, FraserDesign, Loveland, Colorado.

1992a   *Theodore Roosevelt Dam.* Historic American Engineering Record No. AZ-6, FraserDesign, Loveland, Colorado.

1992b   *Stewart Mountain Dam.* Historic American Engineering Record No. AZ-12, FraserDesign, Loveland, Colorado.

More detail regarding the historical archaeology of the dam construction camps in central Arizona may be found in several technical reports.

Ayres, James E., A. E. Rogge, Melissa Keane, Diane L. Douglas, Everett J. Bassett, Diane L. Fenicle, Cindy L. Myers, Bonnie J. Clark, and Karen Turnmire

1994   *The Historical Archaeology of Dam Construction Camps in Central Arizona, Volume 2A: Sites in the Roosevelt Dam Area.* Dames & Moore, Phoenix, Arizona.

Ayres, James E., A. E. Rogge, Everett J. Bassett, Melissa Keane, and Diane L. Douglas

1992   *Humbug! The Historical Archaeology of Placer Mining on Humbug Creek in Central Arizona.* Dames & Moore, Phoenix, Arizona.

Brown, Patricia E.

1978   *Archaeological Investigations at AZ:6:2 (ASU), An Historic Camp on the Banks of the Salt River, Maricopa County, Arizona.* Office of Cultural Resource Management Report No. 32. Arizona State University, Tempe.

Douglas, Diane L., A. E. Rogge, Karen Turnmire, Melissa Keane, James E. Ayres, Everett J. Bassett, and Cindy L. Myers

1994   *The Historical Archaeology of Dam Construction Camps in Central Arizona, Volume 2c: Sites at Other Dams Along the Salt and Verde Rivers.* Dames & Moore, Phoenix, Arizona.

Fenicle, Diane L., James E. Ayres, Everett J. Bassett, Cindy L. Myers, A. E. Rogge, Melissa Keane, and Diane L. Douglas

1994   *The Historical Archaeology of Dam Construction Camps in Central Arizona, Volume 2B: Sites in the New Waddell Dam Area.* Dames & Moore, Phoenix, Arizona.

Hantman, Jeffrey L., and Jeanette A. McKenna

1985   *O'Rourke's Camp: Social Archaeology of an Early Twentieth Century Construction Town.* Anthropological Field Studies No. 7. Arizona State University, Tempe.

Hull-Walski, Deborah A., and James E. Ayres

1989   *The Historical Archaeology of Dam Construction Camps in Central Arizona, Volume 3: Laboratory Methods and Data Computerization.* Dames & Moore, Phoenix, Arizona.

Rogge, A. E., Melissa Keane, and D. Lorne McWatters

1994   *The Historical Archaeology of Dam Construction Camps in Central Arizona, Volume 1: Synthesis.* Dames & Moore, Phoenix, Arizona.

Rogge, A. E., and Cindy L. Myers (editors)

1987a   *A Plan for Archaeological Investigations at Historical Dam Construction Camps in Central Arizona.* Dames & Moore, Phoenix, Arizona.

1987b   *Historical Archaeological Investigations at Dam Construction Camps in Central Arizona: First Annual Report.* Dames & Moore, Phoenix, Arizona.

1988   *Historical Archaeological Investigations at Dam Construction Camps in Central Arizona: Second Annual Report.* Dames & Moore, Phoenix, Arizona.

References Cited

NEWSPAPERS
Arizona Gazette (AG), Phoenix
Arizona Miner (AM), Prescott
Arizona Republican (AR), Phoenix
Arizona Silver Belt (ASB), Globe
Arizona Producer (AP), Phoenix
Associated Arizona Producer (AAP), Phoenix
Phoenix Daily Herald (PDH)

Adams, Robert McC.
  1962   Agriculture and Urban Life in Early Southwestern Iran.
          Science 136:109–122.
Adams, William Y.
  1971   The Development of San Carlos Apache Wage Labor to
          1954. In *Apachean Culture History and Ethnology*, edited
          by Keith Basso and Morris E. Opler, pp. 115–128. Univer-
          sity of Arizona Anthropological Papers No. 21, Tucson.
Anderson, Adrienne B.
  1983   Ancillary Construction on Promontory Summit, Utah:
          Those Domestic Structures Built by Railroad Workers. In
          *Forgotten Places and Things: Archaeological Perspectives on
          American History*, edited by Albert E. Ward, pp. 225–238.
          Contribution to Anthropological Studies No. 3. Center for
          Anthropological Studies, Albuquerque, New Mexico.
Arizona Builder & Contractor
  1938   Wood in a Cement Dam. *Arizona Builder and Contractor*,
          August 1938:7.

Arizona Consolidated Development Company

1906   Placer Lands of the Arizona Consolidated Company (map). Copy on file Central Arizona Project Repository, National Park Service, Tucson.

Ascher, Robert

1974   Tin*Can Archaeology. *Historical Archaeology* 8:7–16.

August, Jack L.

1986   The Future of Western History: The Third Wave. *Journal of Arizona History* 27(2):229–244.

Ayres, James E.

1983   *Archaeological Survey and Evaluation of Structural Components of the Roosevelt Power Canal.* Archaeological Research Services, Tempe, Arizona.

1984   *Rosemont: The History and Archaeology of Post-1880 Sites in the Rosemont Area, Santa Rita Mountains, Arizona.* Arizona State Museum Archaeological Series 147(3). University of Arizona, Tucson.

Bak, P., and K. Chen

1991   Self-Organized Criticality. *Scientific American* 264(1):46–53.

Barnes, Will C.

1988   *Arizona Place Names.* University of Arizona Press, Tucson.

Bartlett, Richard A.

1974   *The New Country: A Social History of the American Frontier, 1776–1890.* Oxford University Press, New York.

Berry, J.W.

1980   Acculturation as Varieties of Adaptation. In *Acculturation: Theory, Models and Some New Findings,* edited by A.M. Padilla, pp. 9–25. Westview Press, Boulder, Colorado.

Bigando, Robert

1989   *Globe, Arizona: The Life and Times of a Western Mining Town.* Mountain Spirit Press, Globe, Arizona.

Bigcrane, Roy, and Thompson Smith

1991   *The Place of Falling Waters* (90 minute video). Salish Kootenai College and Montana Public Television, Bozeman, Montana.

Bilyeu, Edith

1987   Oral Interview. Tape on file at Central Arizona Project Repository, National Park Service, Tucson.

Blanchard, C.J.

1908   Home-Making by the Government: An Account of the Eleven Immense Irrigating Projects to be Opened in 1908. *National Geographic Magazine* 19:250–286.

Bowden, Charles

1977   *Killing the Hidden Waters.* University of Texas Press, Austin.

Boyd, Douglas K., and Meeks Etchieson

1986 *Historic Resources Related to Construction Activities at Elephant Butte Reservoir*. U.S. Bureau of Reclamation, Amarillo, Texas.

Briggs, Alton K.

1974 *The Archaeology of 1882 Labor Camps on the Southern Pacific Railroad, Val Verde County, Texas*. M.A. thesis, Department of Anthropology, University of Texas, Austin.

Brooks, Alison S., Fatimah Linda Collier Jackson, and R. Richard Grinker

1993 Race and Ethnicity in America. *AnthroNotes* 15(3):1–3, 11–15, Smithsonian Institution, Washington, D.C.

Brown, Patricia E.

1978 *Archaeological Investigations at AZ:6:2 (ASU), an Historic Camp on the Banks of the Salt River, Maricopa County, Arizona*. Office of Cultural Resource Management Report No. 32. Arizona State University, Tempe.

Bruder, J. Simon

1975 Historic Papago Archaeology. In *Hecla II and III, An Interpretive Study of Archeological Remains from the Lakeshore Project, Papago Reservation, South Central Arizona*, by Albert C. Goodyear III, pp. 271–337. Arizona State University Anthropological Research Paper No. 9. Tempe.

Buckles, William G.

1976 *Investigations of Historic Communities in Tenmile Canyon, Summit County, Colorado*. Laboratory of Anthropology, University of Southern Colorado, Pueblo.

Cardoso, Lawrence A.

1980 *Mexican Emigration to the United States, 1897–1931*. University of Arizona Press, Tucson.

Carson, Barbara G., and Cary Carson

1983 Things Unspoken: Learning Social History from Artifacts. In *Ordinary People and Everyday Life*, edited by James B. Gardner and George Rollie Adams, pp. 181–203. American Association for State and Local History, Nashville, Tennessee.

Casillas, Michael

1979 *Mexicans, Labor, and Strife in Arizona, 1896–1917*. Unpublished M.A. thesis, Department of History, Arizona State University, Tempe.

Castro, Felipe G.

1992 Acculturation and Cultural Diversity: The Case of Hispanics. In *Harmonizing Arizona's Ethnic & Cultural Diversity*, pp. 47–57. Arizona Town Hall, Phoenix.

Clapp, C.G. (Charley)

1938 Rapid Progress Made on Bartlett Dam. *Arizona Builder & Contractor*, August 1938:5–6.

Cleland, Charles E., and James E. Fitting

    1968   The Crisis of Identity: Theory in Historic Sites Archaeology. In *Conference on Historic Sites Archaeology Papers* 2(2): 124–138.

Costello, Julia G., and Judith Marvin

    1992   *Supplemental Archaeological Survey Report and Historic Study Report for the Highway 395 Alabama Gates Four Lane Project, Inyo County, California.* Foothill Resources, Mokelumne Hill, California.

Cutter, Frank

    1987   Oral interview. Tape on file at Central Arizona Project Repository, National Park Service, Tucson.

Deetz, James

    1977   *In Small Things Forgotten.* Anchor Books, Garden City, New York.

    1988   American Historical Archaeology: Methods and Results. *Science* 239:362–367.

Demos, John

    1970   *A Little Commonwealth: Family Life in Plymouth Colony.* Oxford University Press, New York.

Dill, David B., Jr.

    1987   Breaking the Walnut Grove Dam: An Arizona Catastrophe. *Journal of Arizona History* 28(3):283–305.

Dinnerstein, Leonard, Roger L. Nichols, and David M. Reimers

    1979   *Natives and Strangers: Ethnic Groups and the Building of America.* Oxford University Press, New York.

Dollar, Clyde D.

    1968   Some Thoughts on Theory and Method in Historical Archaeology. In *Conference on Historic Site Archaeology Papers 1967* 2(2):3–10.

Doyel, David E.

    1991   The Hohokam: Ancient Dwellers of the Arizona Desert. In *The Hohokam: Ancient People of the Desert*, edited by David Grant Noble, pp. 3–15. School of American Research Press, Santa Fe, New Mexico.

Dupree, Hunter A.

    1957   *Science in the Federal Government: A History of Policies and Activities to 1940.* Harvard University Press, Cambridge, Massachusetts.

Engineering News-Record

    1938   Rock Slide Kills Three at Bartlett Dam. *Engineering News-Record* (11 Nov) 119:770.

Engineering Record

    1910   Sanitation in Construction Camps of the Catskill Aqueduct. *Engineering Record* 61(14):443–444.

Ferg, Alan (editor)

    1987   *Western Apache Material Culture.* University of Arizona Press, Tucson.

Fink, Leon

1990 American Labor History. In *The New American Labor History*, edited by Eric Foner, pp. 233–250. Temple University Press, Philadelphia.

Fireman, Bert M.

1963 *An Historical Survey of Lake Pleasant Regional Park, Maricopa County, Arizona.* Arizona Historical Foundation, Phoenix.

1982 *Arizona, Historic Land.* Alfred A. Knopf, New York.

Fitch, C.H.

1914 The Mesa-Roosevelt Government Highway. *Reclamation Record* 5(6):217–18.

Fontana, Bernard

1968 A Reply to "Some Thoughts on Theory and Method in Historical Archaeology." In *Conference on Historic Site Archaeology Papers 1967* 2(2):75–78.

Gila County Records

1905– *No. 1527: Ellender Bacon; No. 1275: Jennie Syre; No. 687:*
1911 *Sabarenna Saballas.* Civil Cases, Fifth Judicial District, Territory of Arizona. Department of Library, Archives, and Public Records, Phoenix, Arizona.

1906a *Verdict, Inquisition of the Body of James H. Austin.* Gila County Coroner's Inquest, 19 Mar. Department of Library, Archives, and Public Records, Phoenix, Arizona.

1906b *Verdict, Inquest of Matze, an Indian.* Gila County Coroner's Inquest, 17 Mar. Department of Library, Archives, and Public Records, Phoenix, Arizona.

1909 *Inquisition on Body of Juliana Ultreras.* Gila County Coroner's Inquest, 7 Nov. Department of Library, Archives, and Public Records, Phoenix, Arizona.

Goetzmann, William H.

1966 *Exploration and Empire: The Explorer and Scientist in the Winning of the American West.* Alfred A. Knopf, New York.

Goodwin, Grenville

1935 The Social Divisions and Economic Life of the Western Apache. *American Anthropologist* 37:55–64.

1942 *The Social Organization of the Western Apache.* University of Chicago Press, Chicago.

Gradwohl, David M., and Nancy Osborn

1984 *Exploring Buried Buxton: Archaeology of an Abandoned Iowa Coal Mining Town with a Large Black Population.* Iowa State University Press, Ames.

Granger, Byrd Howell

1983 *Arizona Names (X Marks the Spot).* Falconer Press, Tucson, Arizona.

Grimes, Ronald L.

1986 Desecration of the Dead: An Inter-Religious Controversy. *American Indian Quarterly* 10:305–331.

Gruber, Jacob W.

1984   Artifacts are History: Calver and Bolton in New York. In *The Scope of Historical Archaeology: Essays in Honor of John L. Cotter*, edited by David G. Orr and Daniel G. Crozier. Laboratory of Anthropology, Temple University, Philadelphia.

Haley, James L.

1981   *Apaches: A History and Culture Portrait*. Doubleday, Garden City, New York.

Hamerow, Theodore

1985   The Crisis of the Historical Profession. *Social Science News Letter* 70(2):115–118.

Hantman, Jeffrey L., and Jeanette A. McKenna

1985   *O'Rourke's Camp: Social Archaeology of an Early Twentieth Century Construction Town*. Anthropological Field Studies No. 7. Arizona State University, Tempe.

Harders, Gustav

1912   *Die Heutigen Apachen*. Northwestern Publishing Company, Milwaukee.

1953   *Yaalahn* (originally published in German as *Jaalahn*). Henry C. Nitz, translator. Northwestern Publishing House, Milwaukee.

1958   *Dohaschtida* (originally published in German as *Wille Wider Wille*). Alma Pingel Nitz, translator. Northwestern Publishing House, Milwaukee.

1968   *La Paloma*. Henry C. Nitz, translator. Northwestern Publishing House, Milwaukee.

Harrington, J.C.

1955   Archaeology as an Auxiliary Science in American History. *American Anthropologist* 57:1121–1130.

Haury, Emil W.

1945   *The Excavation of Los Muertos and Neighboring Ruins in the Salt River Valley, Southern Arizona*. Papers of the Peabody Museum of American Archaeology and Ethnology, 24(12). Cambridge, Massachusetts.

1976   *The Hohokam: Desert Farmers and Craftsmen*. University of Arizona Press, Tucson.

Hayes, Jess G.

1968   *Sheriff Thompson's Day: Turbulence in the Arizona Territory*. University of Arizona Press, Tucson.

Hill, Louis C.

1905   Letter to A.P. Davis, Acting Chief Engineer, U.S. Reclamation Service (6 July 1905). Department of the Interior, Record Group 115, General Administrative Files 1902–1919, Box 188, File 447A. National Archives, Washington, D.C.

1906   Letter to F.H. Newell, Chief Engineer U.S. Reclamation Service (30 Aug). Department of the Interior, Record Group

115, General Administrative Files 1902–1919, Box 188, File 447A. National Archives, Washington, D.C.

Hole, Frank, and Robert F. Heizer
1973   *An Introduction to Prehistoric Archeology*. Holt, Rinehart and Winston, New York.

Horton, Elmer
1986   Oral interview. Tape on file at Central Arizona Project Repository, National Park Service, Tucson.

Howard, Jerry B., and Gary Huckleberry
1991   *The Operation and Evaluation of an Irrigation System: The East Papago Canal Study*. Soil Systems Publication in Archaeology No. 18, Phoenix, Arizona.

Hoxie, Norman
1973   *Broken Promises: Indian Assimilation in the 20th Century*. University of Oklahoma Press, Norman.

Imperial, Joaquin
1986   Oral interview. Tape on file at Central Arizona Project Repository, National Park Service, Tucson.

Introcaso, David M.
1984   *The Roosevelt Power Canal and Diversion Dam*. Historic American Engineering Record No. AZ-4. Salt River Project, Phoenix, Arizona.
1988   *Waddell Dam*. Historic American Engineering Record No. AZ-11. Salt River Project, Phoenix, Arizona.
1989   *Mormon Flat Dam*. Historic American Engineering Record No. AZ-14. Salt River Project, Phoenix, Arizona.
1990   *Bartlett Dam*. Historic American Engineering Record No. AZ-25. Salt River Project, Phoenix, Arizona.

Jackson, Donald, and Clayton B. Fraser
1991   *Horseshoe Dam*. Historic American Engineering Record No. AZ-24. FraserDesign, Loveland, Colorado.
1992a   *Theodore Roosevelt Dam*. Historic American Engineering Record No. AZ-6. FraserDesign, Loveland, Colorado.
1992b   *Stewart Mountain Dam*. Historic American Engineering Record No. AZ-12. FraserDesign, Loveland, Colorado.

James, George Wharton
1917   *Reclaiming the Arid West: The Story of the United States Reclamation Service*. Dodd, Mead, and Co., New York.

Johnson, Rich
1977   *The Central Arizona Project: 1918–1968*. University of Arizona Press, Tucson.

Judd, Neil M.
1967   *The Bureau of American Ethnology: A Partial History*. University of Oklahoma Press, Norman.

Kittredge, William
1987   The Secret Life of Those Times. *Montana, The Magazine of Western History* 37(3):84.

LeCount, Al

    1976   *The History of Tonto*. Punkin Center Homemakers, Punkin Center, Arizona.

Lee, Ronald F.

    1970   *The Antiquity Act of 1906*. National Park Service, Washington, D.C.

Leighton, M.O.

    1906   Construction by the U.S. Reclamation Service. *New England Water Works Association* 20:127–151.

Lemisch, Jesse

    1969   The American Revolution Seen from the Bottom Up. In *Towards a New Past: Dissenting Essays in American History*, edited by B.J. Bernstein, pp. 3–45. Random House, New York.

Limerick, Patricia Nelson

    1987   *The Legacy of Conquest: The Unbroken Past of the American West*. W.W. Norton, New York.

    1990   The Rendezvous Model of Western History. In *Beyond the Mythic West*, by Stewart L. Udall, Patricia Nelson Limerick, Charles F. Wilkinson, John M. Volkman, and William Kittredge, pp. 35–59. Peregrine Smith, Salt Lake City, Utah.

    1991   What on Earth is the New Western History? In *Trails Toward a New Western History*, edited by P.N. Limerick, C.A. Milner, II, and C.E. Rankin, pp. 81–88. University Press of Kansas, Lawrence.

    1993   Precedents to Wisdom. *Montana, The Magazine of Western History* 43(4):63–66.

Limerick, Patricia Nelson, Clyde A. Milner, II, and Charles E. Rankin (editors)

    1991   *Trails Toward a New Western History*. University Press of Kansas, Lawrence.

Lipe, William D.

    1992   Summary and Concluding Comments. In *The Sand Canyon Archaeology Project: A Progress Report*, edited by W.D. Lipe, pp. 121–133, Occasional Paper No. 2. Crow Canyon Archaeological Center, Cortez, Colorado.

Luckingham, Bradford

    1989   *Phoenix: History of the Southwestern Metropolis*. University of Arizona Press, Tucson.

Malone, Michael P., and Richard Etulain

    1989   *The American West: A Twentieth Century History*. University of Nebraska Press, Lincoln.

Maricopa County, Arizona, Records

    1896a   *John C. Kellum v. Agua Fria Construction Company*. Maricopa County Superior Court Records, Civil Case No. 2651.

    1896b   *W.K. James v. Agua Fria Construction Company*. Maricopa County Superior Court Records, Civil Case No. 2641.

1896c   *Charles and Leo Goldman v. Agua Fria Construction Company*. Maricopa County Superior Court Records, Civil Case No. 2629.

1896d   *Alex Barsanti v. Agua Fria Construction Company*. Maricopa County Superior Court Records, Civil Case No. 2550.

1896e   *Toohey & George v. Agua Fria Construction Company*. Maricopa Country Superior Court Records, Civil Case No. 2860.

1927a   *Home Accident Insurance Company v. Carl Pleasant*. Maricopa County Superior Court Records, Civil Case No. 26039.

1927b   *Southwest Cotton et al. v. Maricopa County Municipal Water Control District #1 et al.* Maricopa County Superior Court Records, Civil Case No. 23060.

Martin, Russell

1989   *A Story That Stands Like a Dam: Glen Canyon and the Struggle for the Soul of the West*. Henry Holt, New York.

Martin, Russell (editor)

1992   *New Writers of the Purple Sage*. Penguin Books, New York.

Martinelli, Phylis, and Leonard Gordon

1992   The Multiple Dimensions of Cultural Pluralism in Arizona. In *Harmonizing Arizona's Ethnic and Cultural Diversity*, pp. 69–82. Arizona Town Hall, Phoenix.

Masse, W. Bruce

1981   Prehistoric Irrigation Systems in the Salt River Valley, Arizona. *Science* 214:408–415.

McGuire, Randall H.

1982   The Study of Ethnicity in Historical Archaeology. *Journal of Anthropological Archaeology* 1:159–178.

Meredith, H.L.

1968   Reclamation of the Salt River Valley, 1902–1917. *Journal of the West* 7:76–83.

Moody, J. Carroll (editor)

1990   *Perspectives on American Labor History: The Problems of Synthesis*. Northern Illinois Press, Dekalb.

Mooney, James

1965   *The Ghost-Dance Religion and the Sioux Outbreak of 1890* (abridged with introduction by Anthony F.L. Wallace). University of Chicago Press, Chicago. (Originally published in 1896 as Part 2, Fourteenth Annual Report of the Bureau of Ethnology to the Secretary of the Smithsonian Institution, 1892–1893.)

Myres, Sandra L.

1983   Women in the West. In *Historians and the West*, edited by Michael P. Malone, pp. 369–386. University of Nebraska Press, Lincoln.

Newell, Frederick H.

1897   Preface. In *Irrigation Near Phoenix, Arizona*, by A.P. Davis, pp. 9–14. Water Supply and Irrigation Papers of the U.S. Geological Survey No. 2. Government Printing Office, Washington, D.C.

1904   *Proceedings of First Conference of Engineers of the Reclamation Service*. Water Supply and Irrigation Paper No. 93. U.S. Geological Survey, Washington, D.C.

1920   *Water Resources: Present and Future Uses*. Yale University Press, New Haven, Connecticut.

Nials, Fred L., David A. Gregory, and Donald A. Graybill

1989   Salt River Streamflow and Hohokam Irrigation Systems. In *The 1982–1984 Excavations at Las Colinas*, pp. 59–76. Arizona State Museum Archaeological Series 162, Volume 5. University of Arizona, Tucson.

Noble, David Grant (editor)

1991   *The Hohokam: Ancient People of the Desert*. School of American Research Press, Santa Fe, New Mexico.

Noel Hume, Ivor

1961   Preservation of English and Colonial American Sites. *Archaeology* 14(4):250–260.

1975   *Historical Archaeology*. Norton, New York.

Palmer, Ralph F.

1979   *Doctor on Horseback*. Mesa Historical and Archaeological Society, Mesa, Arizona.

Perry, Richard J.

1972   Structural Resiliency and Danger of the Dead: The Western Apache. *Ethnology* 11(4):380–385.

1991   *Western Apache Heritage: People of the Mountain Corridor*. University of Texas Press, Austin.

Pleck, Elizabeth H.

1983   Women's History: Gender as a Category of Historical Analysis. In *Ordinary People and Everyday Life*, edited by James B. Gardner and George Rollie Adams, pp. 51–65. American Association for State and Local History, Nashville, Tennessee.

Price, Ray, and Lee Price

1986   Oral interview. Tapes on file at Central Arizona Project Repository, National Park Service, Tucson.

Rabinowitz, Howard N.

1983   Race, Ethnicity, and Cultural Pluralism in American History. In *Ordinary People and Everyday Life*, edited by James B. Gardner and George Rollie Adams, pp. 181–203. American Association for State and Local History, Nashville, Tennessee.

Rathje, William L., and Michael McCarthy

1977   Regularity and Variability in Contemporary Garbage. In

Research Strategies in Historical Archaeology, edited by
Stanley South, pp. 261–286. Academic Press, New York.

Rathje, William, and Cullen Murphy
  1992   *Rubbish! The Archaeology of Garbage*. HarperCollins, New
          York.

Ready, O.T.
  1910   Construction of the Belle Fourche Dam. *Engineering Rec-
          ord* 61:466–468.

Redfield, Robert, Ralph Linton, and Melville Herskovitz
  1936   Memorandum for the Study of Acculturation for Anthro-
          pology. *American Anthropologist* 38:149–152.

Reisler, Mark
  1976   *By the Sweat of Their Brow: Mexican Immigrant Labor in
          the United States 1900–1940*. Greenwood Press, Westport,
          Connecticut.

Reynolds, William E., S.E. Sobelman, M. McCarthy, and G. Kinkade
  1974   *Archaeological Investigation of the Jackrabbit Mine: Prelim-
          inary Report*. Arizona State Museum Archaeological Series
          No. 39. University of Arizona, Tucson.

Rock, J.
  1981   *Glass Bottles: Basic Identification*. Klamath National Forest,
          Region 5. Department of Agriculture, U.S. Forest Service.
  1984   Cans in the Countryside. In *Historical Archaeology: Journal
          of the Society for Historical Archaeology* 18(2):97–111.

Rogge, A.E.
  1983   *Little Archaeology, Big Archaeology: The Changing Context
          of Archaeological Research*. Ph.D. dissertation, University
          of Arizona and University Microfilms, Ann Arbor, Michi-
          gan.

Rogge, A.E., M. Keane, B. Luckingham, J.E. Ayres, P. Patterson, and
T.W. Bostwick
  1992   *First Street & Madison: Historical Archaeology of the Second
          Phoenix Chinatown*. Intermountain Cultural Resource Ser-
          vices Research Paper No. 9. Dames & Moore, Phoenix,
          Arizona.

Rossillon, Mary P.
  1984   *The Curecanti Archeological Project: The Archeology of
          Marion, an Historic Railroad Camp in Curecanti National
          Recreation Area, Colorado*. Midwest Archeological Center
          Occasional Studies in Anthropology No. 9. National Park
          Service, Lincoln, Nebraska.

Salt River Project Archives
  1904   *Charles W. Williams*. Various letters. Salt River Project Ar-
          chives, Phoenix, Arizona.
  1904–   *List of Subforemen, Foremen, Inspectors, and Timekeep-
  1911   ers; Miscellaneous Contracts; Collections Contracts; Lands
          Flooded by Roosevelt Reservoir (Acres and Cost)*. Salt River
          Project Archives, Phoenix, Arizona.

1906   *Gish Saloon*. Various letters. Salt River Project Archives, Phoenix, Arizona.

1956   *Sallie Berton Pemberton*. File 2453-2. Salt River Project Archives, Phoenix, Arizona.

Salt River Project History Museum

1992   *Jack of All Trades: J.W. Swilling in the Arizona Territory*. Phoenix, Arizona.

Sargent, Charles (editor)

1988   *Metro Arizona*. Biffington Books, Scottsdale, Arizona.

Sauer, Theodore, Harold R. Johne, and Ernst H. Wendland

1992   *To Every Nation, Tribe, Language, and People*. Northwestern Publishing House, Milwaukee, Wisconsin.

Schlesinger, Arthur M.

1991   *The Disuniting of America: Reflections on a Multicultural Society*. Whittle Direct Books, Knoxville, Tennessee.

Schuyler, James D.

1903   *Report on the Water Supply of the Agua Fria River, and the Storage Reservoir Project of the Agua Fria Water and Land Company for Irrigation in the Gila River Valley, Arizona*. Manuscript on file at Arizona Historical Foundation, Tempe.

Schwantes, Carlos A.

1987   The Concept of the Wageworkers' Frontier: A Framework for Future Research. *Western Historical Quarterly* 28(1): 39–55.

Shute, George W.

1909   G.W. Shute (unsigned) to B. Hocker (10 June 1909). Shute Papers, Special Collections, University of Arizona, Tucson.

Smith, Chester A.

1906   Letter to C.M. Fitch, consulting engineer, U.S. Reclamation Service (30 June). Department of the Interior, Record Group 115, General Administrative Files, 1902–1919, Box 188, File 447A. National Archives, Washington, D.C.

1908   Progress on the Roosevelt Dam, Salt River Project, U.S. Reclamation Service. *Engineering News* 60:265–68.

1909   The Building of the Roosevelt Dam. *The Earth* 6(8):2–4.

1910   The Construction of the Roosevelt Dam: An Account of the Difficulties Encountered in Constructing a High Masonry Dam in Arizona. *Engineering Record* 62:756–62.

1912   *Personal Diaries of the Engineer in Charge, Roosevelt Dam, 1903–1912*. Salt River Project Archives, Phoenix, Arizona.

Smith, Karen L.

1986   *The Magnificent Experiment: Building the Salt River Reclamation Project, 1890–1917*. University of Arizona Press, Tucson.

1987   Water, Water Everywhere, Nor. . . In *Arizona at Seventy-Five: The Next Twenty-Five Years*, edited by Beth Luey and

Noel J. Stowe, pp. 149–172. University of Arizona Press, Tucson.

Spicer, Edward H.

1962   *Cycles of Conquest: The Impact of Spain, Mexico, and the United States on the Indians of the Southwest, 1533–1960.* University of Arizona Press, Tucson.

Starr, Jim

1987   Oral Interview. Notes on file at the Central Arizona Project Repository, National Park Service, Tucson.

Stearns, Peter N.

1983   The New Social History: An Overview. In *Ordinary People and Everyday Life,* edited by James B. Gardner and George Rollie Adams, pp. 3–21. American Association for State and Local History, Nashville, Tennessee.

Steele, Rufus

1918   On the Warpath for Fun. *Sunset* 40:52.

Stegner, Wallace

1954   *Beyond the Hundredth Meridian: John Wesley Powell and the Second Opening of the West.* Houghton Mifflin, Boston.

Steiner, Stan

1979   *Fusang: The Chinese Who Built America.* Harper and Row, New York.

Stevens, Joseph E.

1988   *Hoover Dam: An American Adventure.* University of Oklahoma Press, Norman.

Stone, Lyle M., and Scott L. Fedick

1990   *The Archaeology of Two Historic Homestead and Railroad-Related Sites on the Southern Pacific Main Line Near Mobile, Maricopa County, Arizona.* Archaeological Research Services, Inc., Tempe, Arizona.

Teague, George A.

1980   *Reward Mine and Associated Sites: Historical Archaeology on the Papago Reservation.* Western Archaeological Center Publications in Anthropology No. 11. National Park Service, Tucson, Arizona.

1987   *The Archaeology of Industry in North America,* Ph.D. dissertation, Department of Anthropology, University of Arizona, Tucson, and University Microfilms, University of Michigan, Ann Arbor.

1988   Archeology of the Ephemeral: Research Themes for Western Historic Sites. In *Tools to Manage the Past: Research Priorities for Cultural Resources Management in the Southwest,* edited by Joseph A. Tainter and R.H. Hamre, pp. 177–183. General Technical Report No. RM-164. USDA, Forest Service, Fort Collins, Colorado.

Toulouse, Julian H.

1969   *Fruit Jars, A Collector's Manual with Prices.* Thomas Nelson, Nashville, Tennessee.

1971 *Bottle Makers and Their Marks.* Thomas Nelson, New York.

Trimble, Marshall

1986 *Roadside History of Arizona.* Mountain Press, Missoula, Montana.

Turner, Frederick Jackson

1985 *The Frontier in American History.* Reprinted (originally published 1893). University of Arizona Press, Tucson.

1986 The Significance of History. In *Frederick Jackson Turner, Wisconsin's Historian of the Frontier,* edited by Martin Ridge. State Historical Society of Wisconsin, Madison (originally published in *Wisconsin Journal of Education* 21:230–234, 253–256).

United States Bureau of the Census

1913 *Thirteenth Census of the United States Taken in the Year 1910, Abstract of the Census.* Washington, D.C.

United States Bureau of Reclamation

1930– Department of Interior Record Group 115: Bureau of Rec-
1945 lamation Project Correspondence Files. National Archives, Washington, D.C.

1986 *Statistical Compilation of Engineering Features on Bureau of Reclamation Projects.* Engineering and Research Center, Denver, Colorado.

United States Congress, House of Representatives

1911 *Hearings before the Committee on Expenditures on House Resolution #103 to Investigate the Expenditures in the Interior Department.* 7 July:638–642, 702–706.

United States Department of the Interior, Office of Indian Affairs

1902 Report of Agent for San Carlos Agency, by George Corson. In *Annual Report of the Commissioner of the Indian Service.* U.S. Department of the Interior, Office of Indian Affairs.

1904 Report of Agent for San Carlos Agency, by Luther Kelly. In *Annual Report of the Commissioner of the Indian Service.* U.S. Department of the Interior, Office of Indian Affairs.

United States Reclamation Service

1903– *Annual Reports of the Reclamation Service.* Government
1916 Printing Office, Washington, D.C.

1902– *File 8: Labor–General. File 8-1: Mongolian Labor. File 8-2:*
1919 *Labor.* Department of the Interior Record Group 115: General Administrative Files, 1902–1919. National Archives, Washington, D.C.

Wagoner, Jay J.

1970 *Arizona Territory, 1863–1912: A Political History.* University of Arizona Press, Tucson.

Ward, Albert E., Emily K. Abbink, and John R. Stein

1977 Ethnohistorical and Chronological Basis of the Navajo Material Culture. In *Settlement and Subsistence Along the Lower Chaco River: The CGP Survey,* edited by Charles

Reher, pp. 217–278. University of New Mexico Press, Albuquerque.

Way, Peter

1993   Evil Humors and Ardent Spirits: The Rough Culture of Canal Construction Laborers. *Journal of American History* 79(4):1397–1428.

Webb, Walter Prescott

1931   *The Great Plains.* Ginn & Co., Boston.

1964   *The Great Frontier.* University of Texas Press, Austin.

Wegars, Priscilla, and Roderick Sprague

1981   *Archaeological Salvage of the Joso Trestle Construction Camp, 45FR51, Lower Monumental Project.* Anthropological Research Manuscript Series No. 65. University of Idaho, Moscow.

White, Richard

1991   *It's Your Misfortune and None of My Own: A New History of the American West.* University of Oklahoma Press, Norman.

Winters, Joseph C.

1973   Cultural Modifications of the Gila Pima: AD 1697–AD 1846. *Ethnohistory* 29(1):67–77.

Wittfogel, Karl A.

1957   *Oriental Despotism: A Comparative Study of Total Power.* Yale University Press, New Haven, Connecticut.

Worster, Donald

1985   *Rivers of Empire: Water, Aridity and Growth of the American West.* Pantheon, New York.

1992   *Under Western Skies: Nature and History in the American West.* Oxford University Press, New York.

Zarbin, Earl

1984   *Roosevelt Dam: A History to 1911.* Salt River Project, Phoenix, Arizona.

Index

58, 178; laborers on, 77–80, 101, 114, 127, 149

Bean, Curtis Coe, 115

Beardsley, Robert, 152, 153

Beardsley, William, 6, 8, 46, 50 (fig.), 151–53

Beardsley Canal, 47, 105

Boarding houses, 64–65

Boom towns, 33, 35, 170

Boorstein, Daniel, 59

Bottles, 82–84, 110, 153–55

Boyle, Orson, 72, 75, 76

Braddock, Mrs., 64

Broughton, J. C., 103

Bullpen, 37, 42 (fig.), 179 (fig.)

Bureau of American Ethnology (BAE), 7, 22, 23

Bureau of Reclamation, 8–9, 12 (fig.), 54, 56–57. *See also* U.S. Reclamation Service

Burtis, Postmaster, 44, 46

Businesses, 33–34, 64–65, 67–68

Cableways, 95 (fig.), 96–97 (figs.), 152 (fig.)

"California Joe," 71

Camp Dyer, 46–47, 49, 50 (fig.), 64, 97, 106, 131, 155; Jerry Jones at, 151–53

Camp McDowell, 3, 18

Camp Pleasant, 49–51, 54–55 (fig.), 107, 149; archaeology at, 59, 61–63

Camps: Apache, 35, 127, 136–43, 144 (fig.), 148, 154, 160–61. *See also* Construction communities

Camp Verde, 118

Canal companies, 3, 4, 5, 6, 18

Canals, 1–2, 3–4, 18–19, 47, 175

Canning, 81–82

Caretto, John A. B., 156

Carr, Camillo C. C., 18

Carr, Dan, 93 (fig.)

Carrick, Elect, 70

Casey, Ann, 159

Casey, Fred, 160

Casey, John, 158

CCC. *See* Civilian Conservation Corps

Central Arizona Project, 9

Chapman, J. D., 112

Children, 62, 64, 73 (fig.), 74 (fig.), 76, 113

Chinese, 126, 127, 158, 162; artifacts of, 153–55

Civilian Conservation Corps (CCC), 161–62

Clapp, Charley, 114

Climate, 20

Colorado River, 8–9, 11 (fig.), 22

Conchion, John, 100

Conquest, 171, 173

Construction communities, 174, 175–76; archaeological study of, 14, 15–17, 61–63, 80–87; at Bartlett Dam, 56–58, 77–80; at Camp Dyer, 46–47; at Camp Pleasant, 49–51; health and sanitation at, 106–7; at Horseshoe Dam, 58–59, 60 (fig.); at Roosevelt Dam, 33–46, 48 (figs.), 163–64, 177; of Salt River Valley Water Users' Association, 52–55; segregation at, 127–29, 175; size of, 167, 170–71; women in, 63–67

Cottonwood Creek, 94 (fig.)

Cutter, Ernest, 159

Cutter, Frank, 141; life of, 158–62

Daagodighá, 25, 147

Dams, 4, 20, 72, 75; construction of, 7–9, 32–33, 60 (fig.), 89–92, 94–95 (figs.); role of, 5, 12, 17, 175. *See also by name*

Davis Dam, 8

Deaths, 108, 161; accidental, 112–13, 115; alcohol-related, 111–12; in dam construction, 10, 101–5, 114; from diseases, 106–7

Deculturation, 181

Deetz, James, 13–14

Demrick, Almon H., 104–5

Department of Library, Archives, and Public Records, 28

DeVore, W. G., 107

Dillon, W., 103

Discrimination, 129, 131–32, 149, 150–51

Diseases, 106–7

Dohaschtida (Harders), 163, 165

Domestics, 65–66

Drugstores, 109–10, 120

Duarte, Leonica, 113

Duarte, Rafael, 113

Dude ranches, 55–56

Duppa, Darrell, 3

Dyer Diversion Dam, 6, 46–47, 49, 50 (fig.), 126, 151

Early, Scott, 160

Elephant Butte Dam, 14, 127

Engineers, 33, 34, 36–37, 54

Environment, 2; and development, 11–12

Ethnicity, ethnic groups, 68, 125, 170, 175, 176–77; artifacts and, 153–55; classifying, 181–83; of laborers, 99, 126–27, 128 (fig.); stereotyping and, 150–51

Euro-Americans. *See* Anglos

About the Authors

A. E. (GENE) ROGGE holds a doctorate in anthropology from the University of Arizona. For more than twenty years, he has studied the past to identify and preserve important heritage resources as new projects are planned and developed for our modern lives and future uses. Rogge has been director of the Intermountain Cultural Resource Services of Dames & Moore, an international engineering and environmental consulting firm, since 1985. Prior to that, Rogge worked for nine years as an archaeologist for the Bureau of Reclamation. During that time, he managed a study program focused primarily on preserving archaeological information from prehistoric Hohokam sites that lay in the path of the Central Arizona Project, but he also absorbed much of the history of the agency and experienced firsthand how the massive reclamation projects are implemented. Rogge has also promoted archaeology and the appreciation of heritage resources among pre-college students, and he serves on the Arizona Historic Sites Review Committee, which advises the State Historic Preservation Officer and reviews nominations to the National Register of Historic Places.

D. LORNE McWATTERS is an assistant professor of history at Middle Tennessee State University in Murfreesboro, where he teaches courses in public history, historic preservation, cultural resources management, and American history. Crossing the continent from his native British Columbia to study at the University of Florida, he earned a doctorate degree in Latin American history in 1979. While earning his degree, McWatters worked for three years at the Library of Florida History. In 1980, he was appointed visiting assistant professor for three years at the University of Illinois at Urbana-Champaign. Between 1983 and 1993, McWatters was manager and partner of

HMS Associates, a public history consulting firm. While with HMS, he conducted research and wrote on a variety of topics in the American Southeast and Southwest, including the current work on Arizona's dam construction camps. He is currently completing a book on the history of the U.S. Army Corps of Engineers in the Southeast. McWatters' research interests include labor history, environmental history, and the history and preservation of American landscapes and gardens.

MELISSA KEANE is a public historian specializing in interpreting complex historical information for public audiences. Her primary research interest is the history of the twentieth-century American West, and she has used her research and writing skills in a variety of community history projects, including the design of exhibits for the Arizona Historical Society Museum in Tempe. Working with Rogge, she recently coauthored two historical planning documents for the Arizona State Historic Planning Office: *The Chinese in Arizona, 1870–1950* and *Gold and Silver Mining in Arizona, 1848–1945*. Her history of the central Arizona town of Casa Grande during the Great Depression appeared in the *Journal of Arizona History* in the fall of 1991. Keane earned a bachelor's degree from Rice University and a master's degree from the University of Texas, both in anthropology. She is currently a candidate for a master's degree in public history at Arizona State University.

RICHARD P. EMANUEL is a science writer based in Anchorage, Alaska. He has master's degrees in geology and in water resources management from the University of Wisconsin, Madison, and a graduate certificate in science communication from the University of California, Santa Cruz. Prior to becoming a professional writer, he was a hydrologist for eight years with the U.S. Geological Survey in Alaska. His areas of study included computer simulation of groundwater flow and the interactions of volcanoes and glaciers. As a writer, Emanuel has specialized in stories of science told through people. He is a frequent contributor to *Alaska Geographic* quarterly. Since his first trip to Arizona in 1977, he has been a regular visitor to the Sonoran Desert. He is a member of the Society of Professional Journalists and the National Association of Science Writers.